Studies in the Dead Sea Scrolls and Related Literature

Peter W. Flint, Martin G. Abegg Jr., and Florentino García Martínez,
General Editors

The Dead Sea Scrolls have been the object of intense interest in recent years, not least because of the release of previously unpublished texts from Qumran Cave 4 since the fall of 1991. With the wealth of new documents that have come to light, the field of Qumran studies has undergone a renaissance. Scholars have begun to question the established conclusions of the last generation; some widely held beliefs have withstood scrutiny, but others have required revision or even dismissal. New proposals and competing hypotheses, many of them of an uncritical and sensational nature, vie for attention. Idiosyncratic and misleading views of the Scrolls still abound, especially in the popular press, while the results of solid scholarship have yet to make their full impact. At the same time, the scholarly task of establishing reliable critical editions of the texts is nearing completion. The opportunity is ripe, therefore, for directing renewed attention to the task of analysis and interpretation.

Studies in the Dead Sea Scrolls and Related Literature is a series designed to address this need. In particular, the series aims to make the latest and best Dead Sea Scrolls scholarship accessible to scholars, students, and the thinking public. The volumes that are projected — both monographs and collected essays — will seek to clarify how the Scrolls revise and help shape our understanding of the formation of the Bible and the historical development of Judaism and Christianity. Various offerings in the series will explore the reciprocally illuminating relationships of several disciplines related to the Scrolls, including the canon and text of the Hebrew Bible, the richly varied forms of Second Temple Judaism, and the New Testament. While the Dead Sea Scrolls constitute the main focus, several of these studies will also include perspectives on the Old and New Testaments and other ancient writings — hence the title of the series. It is hoped that these volumes will contribute to a deeper appreciation of the world of early Judaism and Christianity and of their continuing legacy today.

Peter W. Flint
Martin G. Abegg Jr.
Florentino García Martínez

REWRITING SCRIPTURE IN SECOND TEMPLE TIMES

Sidnie White Crawford

WILLIAM B. EERDMANS PUBLISHING COMPANY
GRAND RAPIDS, MICHIGAN / CAMBRIDGE, U.K.

Published 2008 by
Wm. B. Eerdmans Publishing Co.
2140 Oak Industrial Drive N.E., Grand Rapids, Michigan 49505 /
P.O. Box 163, Cambridge CB3 9PU U.K.
www.eerdmans.com

Printed in the United States of America

13 12 11 10 09 08   7 6 5 4 3 2 1

Library of Congress Cataloging-in-Publication Data

Crawford, Sidnie White.
Rewriting Scripture in second temple times / Sidnie White Crawford.
p.   cm.   — (Studies in the Dead Sea Scrolls and related literature)
Includes bibliographical references.
ISBN 978-0-8028-4740-9 (pbk.: alk. paper)
1. Dead Sea scrolls.   I. Title.

BM487.C73   2008
296.1'55 — dc22

2007043606

Scripture quotations from the *New Revised Standard Version of the Bible* © 1989 by the Division of Christian Education, National Council of Churches of Christ in the United States of America, are used by permission.

For Frank Moore Cross

מורה צדק

Righteous Teacher

Contents

Preface

The seeds of this project were planted in 1986, when Frank Moore Cross, my "doctor father," invited me to edit for my dissertation seven of the Cave 4 Deuteronomy manuscripts assigned to his lot. It was then that I first encountered 4QDeut^n, a manuscript containing excerpts of a harmonized text of Deuteronomy. What was, I wondered, this strange little manuscript? Then in 1989 John Strugnell invited me to take over his work on the manuscripts at the time called Pentateuchal Paraphrases, and Emanuel Tov graciously accepted me as his junior collaborator on the project. This resulted in our publication of the Reworked Pentateuch manuscripts in 1994. Again I wondered, what were these manuscripts, and what did the people who copied and read them think of them? Finally, Philip Davies of Sheffield Academic Press invited me to contribute a volume on the Temple Scroll to the series Companion to the Qumran Scrolls, which was published in 2000. I raised more questions for myself — how did these different texts fit together, if at all? Thus when Peter Flint asked me to contribute a volume on the "Rewritten Bible" texts from Qumran to this series, I enthusiastically accepted. He has been a most kind editor, waiting patiently to receive a long-delayed manuscript.

In addition to those mentors and colleagues mentioned above, I have many people and institutions to thank. My research assistants at the University of Nebraska-Lincoln, Deanne Hyde Manion, Jessica Buser, Nelson Schneider, and T. Matthew Meyer, rendered invaluable clerical help. Mr. Kenneth Rolling prepared the indices. I gave presentations on various parts of the book at Harvard Divinity School, the University of Wisconsin-Madison, the Society of Biblical Literature, the Colloquium for Biblical Research, Augustana College, the Center of Theological Inquiry, and Princeton Theological Seminary. To all those who participated and gave helpful feedback, I owe my thanks. Several colleagues read and commented on drafts of chapters, which immensely improved the final product: Martin Abegg, Jr., Moshe Bernstein, Dan D. Crawford, Frank Moore Cross, Chip Dobbs-Allsop, Peter Flint, and Benjamin G. Wright III. My husband Dan lived with the project for over five years, offering encouragement, support, and a sharp editorial eye. This volume was completed while I was a member at the Center of Theological Inquiry during the winter and spring of 2005. I would like to thank Wallace Alston, Robert Jenson, Kathi Morley, and the rest of the staff, and the other members of the Center for creating and fostering an ideal environment for scholarship.

Finally, this book is dedicated with gratitude and love to Frank Moore Cross, who for over two decades has been for me the real Righteous Teacher.

SIDNIE WHITE CRAWFORD
Lincoln, Nebraska

Abbreviations

ABD	*Anchor Bible Dictionary*, ed. David Noel Freedman
AbrN	*Abr-Nahrain*
AbrNSup	*Abr-Nahrain: Supplement Series*
BAR	*Biblical Archaeology Review*
BibOr	Biblica et orientalia
BZNW	Beihefte zur Zeitschrift für die neutestamentliche Wissenschaft
CahRB	Cahiers de la Revue Biblique
CBQMS	Catholic Biblical Quarterly Monograph Series
CRINT	Compendia rerum iudicarum ad Novum Testamentum
CSCO	Corpus scriptorum christianorum orientalium
DJD	Discoveries in the Judaean Desert
DSD	*Dead Sea Discoveries*
EDSS	*Encyclopedia of the Dead Sea Scrolls*, ed. Lawrence H. Schiffman and James C. VanderKam
ErIsr	*Eretz-Israel*
frg(s).	fragment(s)
HSS	Harvard Semitic Studies
HTR	*Harvard Theological Review*
HUCA	*Hebrew Union College Annual*
HUCM	Monographs of the Hebrew Union College
JANES	*Journal of the Ancient Near Eastern Society*
JBL	*Journal of Biblical Literature*
JJS	*Journal of Jewish Studies*
JQR	*Jewish Quarterly Review*
JSJ	*Journal for the Study of Judaism*

JSOTSup	Journal for the Study of the Old Testament: Supplement Series
JSPSup	Journal for the Study of the Pseudepigrapha: Supplement Series
LSTS	Library of Second Temple Studies
LXX	Septuagint
MT	Masoretic Text
NIB	*New Interpreter's Bible*
OTP	*The Old Testament Pseudepigrapha*, ed. James H. Charlesworth
RevQ	*Revue de Qumran*
SAOC	Studies in Ancient Oriental Civilizations
SBLEJL	Society of Biblical Literature Early Judaism and Its Literature
ScrHier	Scripta hierosolymitana
SDSSRL	Studies in the Dead Sea Scrolls and Related Literature
SJOT	*Scandinavian Journal of the Old Testament*
SJSJ	Supplements to the Journal for the Study of Judaism
SP	Samaritan Pentateuch
STDJ	Studies on the Texts of the Desert of Judah
StPB	Studia post-biblica
SVTP	Studies in Veteris Testamenti pseudepigrapha
TSAS	Texte und Studien zum antiken Judentum
TZ	*Theologische Zeitschrift*
VTSup	Supplements to Vetus Testamentum

CHAPTER 1

Introduction

It has by now become a commonplace to declare that our understanding of the historical period in Israelite and Jewish religion known as the Second Temple period has been substantially and irrevocably altered by the discovery, decipherment, and dissemination of those ancient Jewish documents known collectively as the Dead Sea Scrolls. But merely because a statement becomes commonplace does not make it any less true, and the Dead Sea Scrolls, a collection of primary Jewish documents written in Hebrew, Aramaic, and Greek and found in a variety of sites along the western shore of the Dead Sea from Khirbet Qumran in the north to Masada in the south, have truly broadened and deepened our understanding of this period of Jewish history[1] in ways too numerous to list here. Two subjects about which the Dead Sea Scrolls give us important new data are the history of the transmission of the text of the Hebrew Bible (the Christian Old Testament) and the ways in which that text was interpreted.

This book is concerned with these two related phenomena, the process of the transmission or handing on of what became known to later Judaism and Christianity as the "Bible" or the "biblical" text by the scribes of the Second Temple period and the methods used to interpret it for contemporary Jews. Although consensus in the field of Hebrew Bible study is hard to come by, most scholars would agree that by the second half of the Second

---

1. The Second Temple period refers to that period of Jewish history which begins with the return of the first exiles from Babylon to Judaea in 538 B.C.E. Scholars usually end the period with the destruction of the Second Temple in Jerusalem by the Romans in 70 C.E., although some would continue the period to the defeat of the Bar Kokhba revolt against Rome in 135 C.E., the final destruction of Jewish national hopes.

Temple period (sometimes called the Greco-Roman period)[2] there existed a body of religious texts, passed down from the ancient kingdoms of Israel and Judah, that the majority of the Jewish community deemed binding for faith and practice. These texts included the Five Books of Moses (i.e., the Torah or Pentateuch), most, if not all, of the Prophets, and at least some of the Writings.[3] As with any religious community, the inheritors of these ancient religious texts, primarily the Jews but also the Samaritans,[4] felt the need to interpret or exegete their sacred texts to ensure their continued relevance in the changing contemporary situation. After the discovery of the Dead Sea Scrolls in the 1940s and 50s, much new evidence came to light on how the exegesis of those sacred texts was carried out by Second Temple Jews.

It was Geza Vermes in 1961 who first identified a group of late Second Temple works as examples of a particular form of interpretation, a group that he identified as a genre dubbed "Rewritten Bible" texts. Vermes defined this genre as characterized "by a close attachment, in narrative and themes, to some book contained in the present Jewish canon of Scripture, and some type of reworking, whether through rearrangement, conflation, or supplementa-

---

2. The Greco-Roman period began with Alexander the Great's conquest of the Persian Empire in 332 B.C.E. Alexander and his successors followed a program of Greek enculturation in the conquered ancient Near East, which produced what is known as the Hellenistic civilization, a fusion of Greek and Near Eastern cultures. Politically, the territory of the former kingdoms of Israel and Judah was first dominated by the Ptolemies (301-197 B.C.E.), then the Seleucids (197-152 B.C.E.). The Hasmonaean dynasty (152-63 B.C.E.) presided over a period of relative political independence for Judaea. The Roman general Pompey's conquest of Judaea (63 B.C.E.) brought the area into the control of Rome and her successors, a situation that continued until the Islamic conquest in the seventh century C.E.

3. The Torah or Law refers to the books of Genesis, Exodus, Leviticus, Numbers, and Deuteronomy. The category Prophets encompasses both historical and prophetic books, i.e., Joshua, Judges, Samuel, and Kings, as well as Isaiah, Jeremiah, Ezekiel, and the Twelve Minor Prophets. The category Writings includes any book that does not fall into the previous two categories, e.g., Psalms, Proverbs, and Job.

4. The term "Jews" refers to that community that considered itself descended from the inhabitants of the old kingdom of Judah who were exiled to Babylon after the destruction of that kingdom in 587 B.C.E. According to their own understanding, they solidified their identity both as an ethnic group and a worshipping community during the exile. In 538 B.C.E, a subgroup returned from exile to Judah, rebuilt the temple of their god Yahweh, and reconstituted a Jewish presence in the land. Jews, however, resided both within the boundaries of the old kingdom of Judah and outside it (the Diaspora).

The term "Samaritans" refers to the community that formed in the old kingdom of northern Israel and its capital, Samaria, after its destruction by the Assyrians in 722 B.C.E. They were also Yahweh worshippers, with their own sanctuary on Mount Gerizim. They were disdained by the Jews as mixed race apostates; Crown, "Samaritans," 817-18.

tion, of the present canonical biblical text."[5] Vermes's original list of works belonging to this genre included Josephus's *Antiquities,* Jubilees, the *Liber Antiquitatum Biblicarum* of Pseudo-Philo, and the *Genesis Apocryphon.* These constitute a wide variety of works, in different languages and from different time periods, and the question arises of whether in fact they constitute a genre. Nevertheless, Vermes's definition remains the starting point for any discussion of this phenomenon, and I will begin by examining his terminology, focusing on the terms "Rewritten" and "Bible."

The word "rewritten" implies the existence of a prior (written) text, which is then revised or recast. The purpose of the revision is exegetical, that is, to explain or interpret the original text for a new (presumably later) audience. According to the evidence of the Hebrew Bible itself, this activity of interpretation by rewriting had begun even before the destruction of the kingdoms. To cite two very obvious examples, the book of Deuteronomy clearly draws on older traditions found in the books of Exodus and Numbers and reworks them, sometimes drastically, to support its own religious and social agenda.[6] Likewise, the Chronicler uses the Deuteronomistic History, primarily the books of Samuel and Kings, and reworks them to forward his exilic vision of the defunct Davidic kingdom as a worshipping community. Michael Fishbane calls this type of interpretive rewriting "inner biblical exegesis."[7]

"Inner biblical exegesis" was carried out by scribes, who were not mere copyists but learned professionals whose task was "the transmission and reinterpretation of received texts and traditions" for later generations.[8] This task involved constant intervention into the received text, intervention that, as far as we can determine, was both expected and accepted as proper scribal activity. The scribes, who may be described as the servants of the text, had a twofold role. First, they had to copy the books of Scripture as exactly as possible, with care for every detail. This is a familiar scribal task. But second, they needed to make the text of Scripture adaptable and relevant to the contemporary situation.[9] They did this by intervention into (or revision of) the text before them. Sometimes this scribal intervention was minor, primarily for purposes of clarification, and appears as what is later described as a gloss in the received text. An example of this would be the updating of archaic place names, as in Josh 18:13: "to the flank of Luz — that is, Bethel." At other times,

5. Vermes, "Bible Interpretation at Qumran," 185-88.

6. See esp. Levinson, *Deuteronomy and the Hermeneutics of Legal Innovation,* for a discussion of how Deuteronomy accomplishes this, and also Najman, *Seconding Sinai,* 10-40.

7. Fishbane, *Biblical Interpretation in Ancient Israel;* "Inner Biblical Exegesis."

8. Fishbane, "Inner Biblical Exegesis," 24.

9. Ulrich, *The Dead Sea Scrolls and the Origins of the Bible,* 11.

however, as in the case of Deuteronomy, this intervention is massive and results in what we would recognize as a new composition. Both types of scribal activity were a sign of reverence for the text, and we may assume that the scribe took his role very seriously. We may also assume that the scribe's audience took his activity seriously. The two activities, exact transcription and intervention for the purposes of exegesis, were not seen as incompatible, but as two sides of the same scribal coin. But the fact that scribal intervention into the text took place at all raises the question, to what degree and for what purposes was this scribal intervention into the sacred text acceptable in the Second Temple period?

We must be careful to realize that the line which we so carefully draw between author and mere copyist was much more fuzzy or even nonexistent in the ancient world. For example, it seems clear that the scribe or scribes who reworked the old Exodus/Covenant traditions now found in Exodus and Numbers meant to create something new, something which became the book of Deuteronomy. What, however, was the purpose of the scribes who dealt with the traditions and texts concerning the prophet Jeremiah? We have the result of their activity in two different but parallel forms of the book of Jeremiah, one form preserved in the version of Jeremiah found in the Septuagint[10] as well as the Qumran manuscripts 4QJer[b, d], and the other, perhaps later, form preserved in Jeremiah as found in the Masoretic Text[11] and 4QJer[a, c]. Here the purpose of the scribes does not seem to have been to create a new composition, but to rework the existing tradition into a new, perhaps updated, edition.[12] Thus we can see that ancient scribal activity took a variety of forms, moving along a spectrum from isolated, small interventions to large-scale, theologically-motivated reworkings. The small interventions are usually unsystematic in character, and a specific theological focus is lacking.[13] The other end of the spectrum, however, contains clear theological programs, which yield new compositions such as Deuteronomy or Chronicles.

The picture we have created of scribes not only copying sacred texts but actually changing them in various ways might be somewhat shocking to

10. The Septuagint refers to the Greek translation of the books of the Hebrew Bible, begun by at least 250 B.C.E., and collected in the Diaspora, primarily in Alexandria, by Greek-speaking Jews as their sacred Scripture.

11. The Masoretic Text is the Hebrew text of the Bible preserved by the Masoretes, Jewish scribes of the Middle Ages who transmitted an ancient consonantal Hebrew text, along with a system of vowel signs and accents. The Masoretic Text is the canonical Bible of Judaism.

12. See Ulrich, *The Dead Sea Scrolls and the Origins of the Bible,* 34-120, for reflections on this phenomenon.

13. Fishbane, *Biblical Interpretation in Ancient Israel,* 84.

modern Jews and Christians, who are used to thinking about their sacred text, the Bible (however that is defined),[14] as inviolate, unchanging. What is there is there and cannot be altered. This attitude pertains both to the text itself (the written word) and the books contained within the two covers called a Bible. However, the evidence we have gathered from the Dead Sea Scrolls, combined with older evidence contained in the Septuagint (LXX) and the Samaritan Pentateuch (SP),[15] indicates that prior to the second century C.E. the text of the Hebrew Bible was not fixed, inviolate and unchanging, but more fluid, subject to scribal intervention for a variety of exegetical purposes. This fluidity was not without limits; at a certain point of change a book would cease to be, say, Genesis, and become something else. But when that "tipping point" occurred is a matter of some debate. If the sacred text is not yet fixed in the late Second Temple period, how can it be characterized as "rewritten"?

A historical perspective is helpful here. Those who have studied the growth of the biblical text throughout the Second Temple period have noted the coalescence of various text-types[16] that become more and more fixed as the period progresses. Frank Moore Cross's classic theory describes three textual families, coming from different geographic regions, of which the main exemplars were the Masoretic Text (Babylonia), the Samaritan Pentateuch (Old Palestinian), and the Septuagint (Egypt).[17] Later scholars have rejected the notion of geographic location, choosing to focus on textual characteristics. Thus Emanuel Tov argues that two distinct groupings of texts can be recognized, a proto-rabbinic group[18] and a pre-Samaritan group; however,

14. Although both Jews and Christians use the English word "Bible" to denote their canon of sacred Scriptures, the meaning behind the term differs between the two communities, as well as for different communities within Christianity. In Judaism, the 24 books of the *Torah* (Law), *Nevi'im* (Prophets), and *Ketubim* (Writings), or *TaNaK*, is what is referred to by the English word Bible. The Christian community took over that collection, naming it the Old Testament, and added to it the books of the New Testament. In addition, Orthodox Christians and Roman Catholics have a larger collection of Jewish sacred texts in their Old Testaments; those books that do not appear in Jewish Bibles are grouped together under the term Apocrypha.

15. The Samaritan Pentateuch is that version of the Torah or Pentateuch preserved as canonical by the Samaritan community.

16. See the definitions of "text-type" by Ulrich and Davila in Chapter 2 below.

17. Cross, "The History of the Biblical Text," 193-95.

18. Also called the proto- or pre-Masoretic group. The term "proto-rabbinic" better describes this group of texts, since it is from these manuscripts that the individual books that became canonical in the rabbinic period (the *textus receptus*) were descended. These texts were later vocalized by the Masoretes in the medieval period, hence the term "Masoretic Text." It is important to realize, however, that each book that later made up the Rabbinic Bible had a separate textual history; the books do not share a specific set of textual characteristics. All that binds them to-

many texts fall outside those two groupings and are considered nonaligned.[19] Eugene Ulrich has focused on the appearance of parallel editions of some books, emphasizing that in Second Temple Judaism, it was the book, rather than its specific textual form, that was considered sacred.[20]

Whichever theory of textual development one embraces, it becomes clear from studying the manuscripts of the various sacred books recovered from the Judaean desert that by the late Second Temple period their textual forms were becoming fixed. A certain amount of flux and change was still permissible, and it was still acceptable to have different editions of the same book in circulation. However, this is what Kister has called a "post-classical" period, where Scripture is already available to be commented on.[21] Thus, when a learned scribe developed a received text through innerbiblical exegesis, a point of comparison was readily available, already in circulation. The question of whether or not this was a new work, and whether or not it carried the same authority as the received text, became a point of disagreement among various groups of Jews at the time.

Turning to Vermes's use of the terms "Bible" and "canonical" in his definition, a scholarly consensus now exists that in the Second Temple period there was no "canon" of sacred Scripture.[22] The Jewish community did not promulgate an official canon of Scripture until after the end of the Second Temple period. There was no "Bible" in Second Temple Judaism. Thus, it is an anachronism to use "Bible" or its adjective "biblical" to describe religious texts in that period, even if they became biblical in later times. However, once we have made the statement that there was no Bible in Second Temple Judaism, it is equally clear that, especially in the second half of the period, there was a generally accepted body of sacred literature that was considered by Jews to be uniquely authoritative, ancient in origin, and binding on the community for doctrine and practice. In this book, we will use the fairly generally accepted terms "Scripture(s)" and "scriptural" to refer to these sacred texts in

---

gether as a group is their eventual selection as the *textus receptus* of the Rabbinic Bible. The textual history of each book must be considered separately; Ulrich, *The Dead Sea Scrolls and the Origins of the Bible*, 32, 113-15.

19. Tov, "Scriptures: Texts," 833-34. Tov acknowledges that a few particular texts lie very close to the presumed Hebrew *Vorlage* of the Septuagint. See also "The Biblical Texts from the Judaean Desert — An Overview and Analysis of the Published Texts," 137-44.

20. Ulrich, *The Dead Sea Scrolls and the Origins of the Bible*, 93.

21. Kister, "A Common Heritage," 101-2.

22. Flint defines a canon as "the closed list of books that was officially accepted retrospectively by a community as supremely authoritative and binding for religious practice and doctrine"; "Scriptures in the Dead Sea Scrolls," 270.

Second Temple Judaism.[23] These texts included the five books of the Torah or Pentateuch, and all or almost all of the entire prophetic corpus.[24] The status of the corpus known as the Writings is much more uncertain. How do we determine the authoritative status of religious texts in Judaism during the Second Temple period? While the discovery of the Dead Sea Scrolls has increased our ability to answer that question, some ambiguity still remains.

Prior to the discovery of the Scrolls, we had very little contemporary evidence concerning which books had gained scriptural status. Several Jewish or early Christian works do give evidence that, for at least some groups of Jews in the Second Temple period, certain books had obtained scriptural status.[25] Ben Sira, the early second-century B.C.E. sage, in his list of Israel's ancestors in chs. 44-50 of his eponymous book (The Wisdom of Jesus ben Sira, or Ecclesiasticus), mentions figures and events from most books in what later became the Jewish Bible, in their familiar order. This list may indicate that the books in which these figures and events appear had obtained scriptural status by *ca.* 180 B.C.E. Ben Sira's grandson, in his prologue to his Greek translation of his grandfather's book (after 132 B.C.E.), refers to "the Law and the Prophets and the other books." The meaning of "Law" and "Prophets" seems fairly clear and probably coincides with our understanding of those terms. However, the phrase "other books" is very ambiguous, and we cannot be certain what books Ben Sira's grandson would have included in the term, or even if he would have granted them scriptural status.

Other pieces of evidence come from the end of the Second Temple period. The author of Luke-Acts (*ca.* 90 C.E.) refers to the Law (or Moses) and the Prophets (Luke 16:16, 29, 31; 24:27; Acts 26:22; 28:23) and once also to the Psalms (Luke 24:44). 4 Ezra 14:23-48 (*ca.* 100 C.E.) speaks of 94 inspired books, of which 24 are public and 70 hidden. The 24 likely coincide with the canonical list of the Jewish Bible. Finally, Josephus, writing *ca.* 90-100 C.E., lists 22 books that are "justly accredited": five books of Moses, 13 prophetic books, and four books of hymns and precepts (*C. Ap.* 1.37-43). Except for the five books of Moses (the Torah), Josephus's list is vague, and scholars disagree over which books should be included.

The Qumran collection of the Dead Sea Scrolls has also shed some light on the subject. The Qumran collection refers to those scrolls that came from the 11 caves in the vicinity of Khirbet Qumran, on the northwest corner

---

23. Flint, "Scriptures in the Dead Sea Scrolls," 272.

24. The Samaritan community only accepted the Five Books of Moses, or Torah, as authoritative.

25. Ulrich, "Canon," 118-19.

of the Dead Sea. These scrolls, almost entirely religious in nature, form a co-herent collection that belonged to a particular group within Judaism in the late Second Temple period, a group that differentiated itself from other Jews in matters of practice and doctrine. This group was in all probability the Essenes or a subset of them.[26] The manuscripts from Qumran date, according to paleographic criteria, from *ca.* 250 B.C.E. to *ca.* 68 C.E. Thus they give us a good snapshot of what religious texts were in circulation and were collected by at least one group of Jews in the Second Temple period. By analyzing this collection we can determine which texts had scriptural status for the Qumran community.

The first question we should ask is whether there are any internal indicators that the Qumran community had a scriptural collection. The document *Miqṣat Maʿaśĕ ha-Tôrāh* indicates an awareness of such a collection: "[And] we have [written] to you so that you may study (carefully) the book of Moses and the books of the Prophets and (the writings of) David . . ." (4QMMT C 10).[27] As we found in the citations from Ben Sira and the others, this quote leaves us with uncertainty: "the book of Moses" is certainly the Torah, but does the singular word "book" indicate that by the time of 4QMMT (mid-second century B.C.E.) the Torah was considered one work, instead of five separate books? The rest of the Qumran collection would militate against such a conclusion, since the five books of the Pentateuch are individually preserved in many manuscripts. However, the Pentateuch or Torah is also often considered and treated as a whole (see Chapter 2). The phrase "books of the Prophets" points to the canonical group known as the Prophets, but did it include all the books that later became canonical? Did it include some books that were later rejected? Finally, the last category, "David," is the most obscure. Certainly it includes the Psalms, but did it include anything else? Clearly we must look for another way to determine the scriptural status of the works preserved in the Qumran collection.

The method for carrying out such an analysis is fairly well agreed. To be identified as scripture for a particular community, in this case the Qumran community, a work should meet some or all of the following criteria.[28] (1) The work is quoted or alluded to as having special authority or scriptural status. Formulae such as "thus says the Lord" or "as it is written" are helpful indicators. (2) The work is the subject of a commentary, such as *Pesher*

---

26. For a good defense of this position, see VanderKam and Flint, *The Meaning of the Dead Sea Scrolls,* 240-50.

27. Qimron and Strugnell, *Miqṣat Maʿaśe ha-Tôrâh,* 58-59.

28. VanderKam, *The Dead Sea Scrolls Today,* 150; Flint, "Scriptures in the Dead Sea Scrolls," 293-300.

Nahum or *Pesher Habakkuk*. (3) The work claims for itself divine authority, for example by attribution to Moses. (4) If the work is preserved in a large number of copies, that may point to scriptural status or at least special importance. (This is the weakest criterion, since the manuscripts preserved in the Qumran collection are at least partly a matter of historical accident.)

According to the criteria set out above, we can make definitive statements about the scriptural status of certain books from the Qumran collection. For example, Deuteronomy was without doubt considered scriptural and authoritative by the Qumran community. It is quoted or alluded to extensively throughout the manuscript collection, it presents itself as divinely authorized, coming from the mouth of Moses, and it is preserved in 31 copies. On the other hand, it is equally certain that the book of Esther was not considered scriptural at Qumran. No scrap of the book was preserved at Qumran; it is not quoted or alluded to in any other Qumran document.[29] Most tellingly, the festival of Purim is not mentioned in any of the calendar texts preserved at Qumran and evidently was not celebrated there.

A preliminary list of books that had obtained scriptural status at Qumran would include the Torah, most, if not all, of the Prophets, and Psalms, Proverbs, Job, and Daniel. Ecclesiastes, Ezra/Nehemiah, Chronicles, and Song of Solomon are uncertain; Esther was not included. The list of sacred Scriptures also included works that were not later admitted into the Jewish or (most) Christian canons: 1 Enoch,[30] Jubilees (see below, Chapter 4), and possibly some others.

On the basis of all that has been said above, we can see that there are difficulties with Vermes's genre name "Rewritten Bible." The term "Bible," as is the related term "canon," is anachronistic in the Second Temple period. The term "rewritten" is hard to reconcile with the fact that we do not begin to recognize a fixed text until relatively late in the period. However, once these difficulties are understood and the term "Scripture" is substituted for "Bible," is Vermes's genre classification still useful to explain a certain group of texts from the Second Temple period? I will argue that it is and that the "Rewritten Scripture" category can be distinguished from other types of exegetical works found in the Qumran library. First, I will examine the views of four scholars

29. *Pace* Talmon, "Was the Book of Esther Known at Qumran?"

30. 1 Enoch is a collection of pseudepigraphical works composed in the name of Enoch, son of Jared (Gen 5:21-24). Originally composed in Aramaic, 1 Enoch was translated into Greek and hence into Ethiopic, the language of the Abyssinian Orthodox Church. Fragments of 17 Aramaic manuscripts and possibly one Greek manuscript of 1 Enoch were found at Qumran. The traditions found in 1 Enoch were extremely important for one stream of tradition and interpretation found in Second Temple Judaism.

who have contributed to the discussion concerning Rewritten Scripture since Vermeš first used the phrase "Rewritten Bible" in 1961: Philip Alexander, Moshe Bernstein, George Brooke, and Emanuel Tov. Then I will proffer my own understanding and definition of the category.[31]

Philip Alexander points out that the term "Rewritten Bible" is often used loosely, even carelessly, with the result that everyone comes up with different lists when defining the category. He aims to produce a more stringent definition of the genre, for which he includes the following nine points:[32]

1. Rewritten Bible texts are narratives, which follow a sequential, chronological order.
2. They are . . . freestanding compositions, which replicate the form of the biblical books on which they are based.
3. These texts are not intended to replace, or to supersede the Bible.
4. Rewritten Bible texts cover a substantial portion of the Bible.
5. Rewritten Bible texts follow the Bible serially, in proper order, but they are highly selective in what they represent.
6. The intention of the texts is to produce an interpretative reading of Scripture.
7. The narrative form of the text means . . . that they can impose only a single interpretation on the original.
8. The limitations of the narrative form also preclude making clear the exegetical reasoning.
9. Rewritten Bible texts make use of non-biblical traditions and draw on non-biblical sources.

As a result of this more stringent definition, he suggests the following list of works as belonging to the genre: Jubilees, Genesis Apocryphon, the *Liber Antiquitatum Biblicarum* of Pseudo-Philo, and Josephus's *Antiquities*.[33] He does not appear to consider this list closed or final. Alexander arrives at essentially the same list as Vermes, but his more rigid definition helps to define

---

31. Although George W. E. Nickelsburg ("The Bible Rewritten and Expanded"; "Stories of Biblical and Early Post-Biblical Times") and Daniel Harrington ("The Bible Rewritten [Narratives]") each use the term "Rewritten Bible" in their surveys of Second Temple Jewish literature, both have a broader definition of the term than do I or any of the four scholars mentioned above. As will be seen, I embrace a narrower definition of the term and will make a distinction between Rewritten Scripture and parabiblical literature. See also Bernstein, "'Rewritten Bible'," 176-80.

32. Alexander, "Retelling the Old Testament," 116-18.

33. Alexander, "Retelling the Old Testament," 99-100.

the category more clearly by excluding works such as 1 Enoch, which is related to the text of Genesis through the character of Enoch but which departs radically from Genesis.

Moshe Bernstein[34] is interested in retaining Vermes's genre definition, but wishes to broaden its scope beyond the narrative to embrace legal texts as well. This broadening would allow the inclusion of the Temple Scroll in the category. In addition, Bernstein argues that care needs to be exercised concerning which texts are included in the genre. First, he would exclude any texts meant to be "biblical" texts or "biblical" translations; this would exclude, for example, the Samaritan Pentateuch and the Palestinian Targums. He acknowledges, however, that it is sometimes impossible to make a hard and fast distinction between "biblical" and "nonbiblical": "one group's 're-written Bible' could very well be another's biblical text!"[35] He also raises the question of degree: "how different from the biblical original need a text be before we call it 'rewritten Bible'?"[36] For Bernstein, the definition and thus the list of works to be included in the category is more subjective than it is for Alexander. According to Bernstein, a Rewritten Bible text is characterized by "comprehensive or broad scope rewriting of narrative and/or legal material with commentary woven into the fabric implicitly, but perhaps *not* merely a biblical text with some superimposed exegesis."[37]

George Brooke argues that, rather than thinking in terms of a genre, we should think of "rewritten scriptural texts" (his preferred term) as a category. In that category would fall "any representation of an authoritative scriptural text that implicitly incorporates interpretative elements, large or small, in the retelling itself."[38] Under that rubric would fall versions of texts that later became canonical in certain communities, such as the Samaritan Pentateuch, which is a harmonized and expanded edition of the Pentateuch. That is precisely the danger that Bernstein warns of in his comment that one group's rewritten Bible may be another's canonical text. Brooke does acknowledge the problem by noting that a neat separation between "scripture" and "rewritten" is impossible; he uses the term "sliding scale" to talk about degrees of rewriting.[39]

Brooke proposes the following definition for a rewritten scriptural text: it is "essentially a composition which shows clear dependence on a scriptural

34. Bernstein, "'Rewritten Bible.'"
35. Bernstein, "'Rewritten Bible,'" 175.
36. Bernstein, "'Rewritten Bible,'" 189.
37. Bernstein, "'Rewritten Bible,'" 195.
38. Brooke, "Rewritten Bible," 777.
39. Brooke, "The Rewritten Law, Prophets and Psalms," 36.

text."[40] Further refining this rather general description, he goes on to list the following characteristics:

1. The source is thoroughly embedded in its rewritten form not as explicit citation but as running text.
2. The dependence of a rewritten scriptural text on its source is also such that the order of the source is followed extensively.
3. The dependence of a rewritten scriptural text on its source is also such that the content of the source is followed relatively closely without very many major insertions or omissions.
4. The original genre or genres stays much the same.
5. And finally, the new texts are not composed to replace the authoritative sources which they rework.[41]

Emanuel Tov makes a strong distinction between "biblical" texts, which have authoritative status, and "rewritten Bible compositions," which do not. "It is not the amount of exegesis . . . which counts, but the purpose of the manuscript under investigation."[42] Tov's position, based on the manuscript evidence from the Qumran collection, is that by the late Second Temple period a clear distinction could be made by the community between an authoritative, scriptural text and a rewritten version thereof. However, the problem with attempting to make this distinction is again found in Bernstein's warning. Tov himself acknowledges that "the definition of what constitutes a rewritten Bible text is actually less clear now than it was a few years ago."[43] The question of authority or scriptural status will prove to be a thorny one, since, as we shall see, a salient characteristic of many of the works we would place in the category Rewritten Scripture is the claim to divine authority and therefore scriptural status.

My own understanding of the use of inner scriptural exegesis in works of the late Second Temple period to produce texts with certain identifiable characteristics is informed by all of these scholars, especially Brooke and Bernstein. Rather than use Vermes's problematic term "Rewritten Bible," I prefer (with Brooke) "rewritten scriptural texts" or "Rewritten Scripture." These Rewritten Scriptures constitute a category or group[44] of texts which are

40. Brooke, "The Rewritten Law, Prophets and Psalms," 32.
41. Brooke, "The Rewritten Law, Prophets and Psalms," 32-33.
42. Tov, "Rewritten Bible Compositions and Biblical Manuscripts," 334.
43. Tov, "Rewritten Bible Compositions and Biblical Manuscripts," 337.
44. By the terms "group" or "category" I refer to a set of texts sharing common textual characteristics, which are both closely related internally and different from other textual enti-

characterized by a close adherence to a recognizable and already authoritative base text (narrative or legal) and a recognizable degree of scribal intervention into that base text for the purpose of exegesis. Further, the rewritten scriptural text will often (although not always) make a claim to the authority of revealed Scripture, the same authority as its base text. The receiving community will not necessarily accept such a claim. This definition is fairly broad, so I would refine it by introducing the concept of a spectrum of texts (similar to Brooke's "sliding scale").

At one end of the spectrum lie scriptural texts that are recognizably authoritative across groups, although different editions may become canonical for different subgroups. Thus, both the proto-Rabbinic text of the Torah and the texts of the pre-Samaritan group would fall at this end of the spectrum, even though the pre-Samaritan group is clearly a harmonized and expanded version of a prior base text. This is because both versions make the same claim to Mosaic authority and both were adopted by religious communities as their canonical scriptures. The exegetical technique chiefly utilized by the pre-Samaritan group of texts is the technique of harmonization, whereby, if a contradiction or omission is perceived in a certain passage of the base text, material from another part of the base text is introduced into that passage, to smooth out contradictions and bring the two parts into harmony. That is, exegesis is accomplished by manipulation of the existing base text only; nothing from outside the existing base text is utilized. In Chapter 2 we will discuss scriptural texts that later became canonical in some religious community and demonstrate the evidence for scribal intervention in them. We will investigate particularly the technique of harmonization in the pre-Samaritan group of texts.

The next area along the spectrum is occupied by texts whose scribal intervention does utilize material from outside the existing base text, but without the intention thereby of creating a new composition. These texts are making the same claim to authority as their base texts, but whether these claims were universally accepted is a matter of some doubt. The status of these texts, and the proper nomenclature to be used when discussing them, is hotly debated, as we shall see in Chapter 3. Chapter 3 concentrates on the texts named "Reworked Pentateuch," which move beyond the harmonistic exegesis of the pre-Samaritan group of texts by adding material not found in the base text into the reworked text. The claims to authority by the Re-

---

ties; see Tov, "Groups of Biblical Texts Found at Qumran," 86. A group or category may have works of different genres within it, such as narrative works (Jubilees) or legal works (the Temple Scroll).

worked Pentateuch texts are clear, but their status as Scripture in Second Temple Judaism is debatable.

Next on the spectrum come works in which the scribal manipulation of the base text is so extensive that a recognizably new work is created. In these works the base text is still clearly identifiable, but the new work has a separate purpose or theological *tendenz*. The claim to universal authority is the same as that of the base text, but it is only accepted by smaller subgroups, if at all. Chapters 4 and 5 select two examples of Rewritten Scripture texts that become recognizably new compositions, while making the same claim to divine authority as their base texts. One work is narrative (Jubilees), while the other is legal (the Temple Scroll).

At the far end of the spectrum are works that fall only peripherally within the bounds of our definition. These works have a recognizable authoritative base text, and they rework that base text using many of the techniques of innerscriptural exegesis, but they do not claim the authority of the base text, nor did any community accord it to them. They may also be translations, which remove them even further from the base text. The Genesis Apocryphon, an Aramaic work that is an example of this type of composition, is the subject of Chapter 6. The book closes, in Chapter 7, with a look at a work that combines Rewritten Scripture and the "lemma plus commentary" style of interpretation. This latter style of interpretation is familiar to us, since it is the style found in most contemporary Bible commentaries. A passage of Scripture is quoted, and then a separate exegetical comment is given. There is a clear distinction made between the sacred text and the interpretation of it. The work that is the subject of Chapter 7, 4QCommentary on Genesis, signals a transition away from the old interpretative method of rewriting within a scriptural base text to this fixed text, "lemma plus commentary" style of interpretation which became characteristic of rabbinic Judaism and early Christianity.

Finally, a very prominent group of texts in the Qumran collection falls completely outside the boundaries of our definition and will not be considered in this volume. These are what I term the "parabiblical" texts. These texts use a passage, event, or character from a scriptural work as a "jumping off" point to create a new narrative or work. Examples of parabiblical texts found at Qumran include 1 Enoch and the pseudo-Ezekiel texts and, from outside Qumran, works like The Life of Adam and Eve and Joseph and Asenath.[45]

---

45. Many of these works fall within the boundaries of Nickelsburg's and Harrington's definitions. See also the classification of Lange, who includes "Rewritten Bible" under the larger term "Parabiblical Texts"; "Annotated List of the Texts from the Judaean Desert," 117-18.

These parabiblical texts seem to have had a variety of purposes, some with a definite theological agenda. While in some cases they may have made a claim to authority, their collective status in late Second Temple Judaism is extremely murky.

I have chosen for each chapter examples from the Pentateuch, as these examples are the most clear and the most numerous; however, they are certainly not meant to be exhaustive. All of these examples were located in the caves of Qumran and formed part of the Qumran Essene library. Therefore, in addition to investigating the method of interpretation and the scribal techniques used in rewriting, we will want to ask whether or not there is any particular line of scribal interpretation manifest in these works. The preliminary answer is "yes." The interpretive tradition embraced by the texts we will investigate, and texts related to them, is a *written* tradition with particular priestly concerns. These concerns embrace the temple and all that pertains to it, including the proper ritual calendar and the correct performance of the cult and the festival rituals. In addition, the tradition has a strong interest in matters of purity and impurity, in which the laws of levitical and priestly purity are extended to cover the entire people of Israel. This priestly-levitical line of interpretation, which appears in works that were composed at least as early as the third century B.C.E., relies on a set of scriptural passages concerning the role of Levi and his heirs the priests in interpretation, teaching, and instruction: Deut 17:8-13; 33:10; and Mal 2:4-7.[46] These scriptural passages form the basis for a priestly scribal tradition of written interpretation of Scripture held in the hands of the priests. This tradition reaches its zenith in the works of the Qumran community, which embraces a divinely revealed, authoritative interpretation of Scripture promulgated by Zadokite priests, of whom the Teacher of Righteousness was probably one.[47] This tradition is opposed to the line of interpretation embraced by the Pharisees and the later rabbis,[48] as shown by the almost complete absence of Pharisaic traditions in the Qumran manuscripts.[49] We will watch for evidence of this priestly-levitical exegetical tradition in the chapters that follow.

46. Kugel, "Ancient Biblical Interpretation and the Biblical Sage," 6-7.

47. VanderKam and Flint, *The Meaning of the Dead Sea Scrolls*, 263. The Teacher of Righteousness appears in the Damascus Document and a few *pesharim*, works belonging to the Qumran community, as an important leader of the movement and its inspired interpreter of Scripture.

48. It is interesting to note that the Pharisaic chain of tradition in *m. Abot* 1 does not include a single identified priest; Baumgarten, "Literacy and the Polemics Surrounding Biblical Interpretation," 33.

49. VanderKam and Flint, *The Meaning of the Dead Sea Scrolls*, 280.

Bibliography

Alexander, Philip S. "Retelling the Old Testament." In *It Is Written: Scripture Citing Scripture,* ed. D. A. Carson and H. G. M. Williamson, 99-121. Cambridge: Cambridge University Press, 1988.

Baumgarten, Albert I. "Literacy and the Polemics Surrounding Biblical Interpretation in the Second Temple Period." In *Studies in Ancient Midrash,* ed. James L. Kugel, 27-42. Cambridge, MA: Harvard University Press, 2001.

Bernstein, Moshe. "'Rewritten Bible': A Generic Category which has Outlived Its Usefulness?" *Textus* 22 (2005) 169-96.

Brooke, George J. "Rewritten Bible." In *EDSS,* 2:777-81.

———. "The Rewritten Law, Prophets and Psalms: Issues for Understanding the Text of the Bible." In *The Bible as Book: The Hebrew Bible and the Judaean Desert Discoveries,* ed. Edward D. Herbert and Emanuel Tov, 31-40. London: British Library and New Castle, DE: Oak Knoll, 2002.

Crawford, Sidnie White. "How Archaeology Affects the Study of Texts: Reflections on the Category 'Rewritten Bible' at Qumran." In *Caves of Enlightenment: Proceedings of the American Schools of Oriental Research Dead Sea Scrolls Jubilee Symposium (1947-1997),* ed. James H. Charlesworth, 39-54. North Richland Hills, TX: BIBAL, 1998.

———. "The Rewritten Bible at Qumran." In *The Bible and the Dead Sea Scrolls,* ed. James H. Charlesworth, 1: *The Hebrew Bible and Qumran,* 173-95. North Richland Hills, TX: BIBAL, 2000.

———. "The 'Rewritten Bible' at Qumran: A Look at Three Texts." In *Frank Moore Cross Volume,* ed. Baruch Levine, Philip J. King, Joseph Naveh, and Ephraim Stern. *ErIsr* 26 (1999) 1*-8*.

Cross, Frank Moore. "The History of the Biblical Text in the Light of Discoveries in the Judaean Desert." In *Qumran and the History of the Biblical Text,* ed. Cross and Shemaryahu Talmon, 177-95. Cambridge, MA: Harvard University Press, 1975.

Crown, Alan D. "Samaritans." In *EDSS,* 2:817-18.

Davila, James R. "Text-Type and Terminology: Genesis and Exodus as Test Cases." *RevQ* 16 (1993-95) 3-37.

Fishbane, Michael. *Biblical Interpretation in Ancient Israel.* Oxford: Clarendon, 1985.

———. "Inner Biblical Exegesis: Types and Strategies of Interpretation in Ancient Israel." In *Midrash and Literature,* ed. Geoffrey H. Hartman and Sanford Budick, 19-37. New Haven: Yale University Press, 1986.

Flint, Peter. "Scriptures in the Dead Sea Scrolls: The Evidence from Qumran." In *Emanuel: Studies in Hebrew Bible, Septuagint, and Dead Sea Scrolls in Honor* of *Emanuel Tov*, ed. Shalom M. Paul, Robert A. Kraft, Lawrence H. Schiffman, and Weston W. Fields, 269-304. VTSup 94. Leiden: Brill, 2003.

Harrington, Daniel. "The Bible Rewritten (Narratives)." In *Early Judaism and Its Modern Interpreters*, ed. Robert A. Kraft and G. W. E. Nickelsburg, 239-47. Atlanta: Scholars, 1986.

Kister, Menahem. "A Common Heritage: Biblical Interpretation at Qumran and Its Implications." In *Biblical Perspectives*, ed. Michael E. Stone and Esther G. Chazon, 101-11. STDJ 28. Leiden: Brill, 1998.

Kugel, James L. "Ancient Biblical Interpretation and the Biblical Sage." In *Studies in Ancient Midrash*, 1-26. Cambridge, MA: Harvard University Press, 2001.

Lange, Armin, with Ulrike Mittmann-Reichert. "Annotated List of the Texts from the Judaean Desert Classified by Content and Genre." In *The Texts from the Judaean Desert: Indices and an Introduction to the Discoveries in the Judaean Desert Series*, ed. Emanuel Tov, 115-64. DJD 39. Oxford: Clarendon, 2002.

Levinson, Bernard M. *Deuteronomy and the Hermeneutics of Legal Innovation*. New York: Oxford University Press, 1997.

Najman, Hindy. *Seconding Sinai: The Development of Mosaic Discourse in Second Temple Judaism*. SJSJ 77. Leiden. Brill, 2003.

Nickelsburg, George W. E. "The Bible Rewritten and Expanded." In *Jewish Writings of the Second Temple Period*, ed. Michael E. Stone, 89-156. CRINT 2/2. Assen: Van Gorcum and Philadelphia: Fortress, 1984.

————. "Stories of Biblical and Early Post-Biblical Times." In *Jewish Writings of the Second Temple Period*, ed. Michael E. Stone, 33-87. CRINT 2/2. Assen: Van Gorcum and Philadelphia: Fortress, 1984.

Qimron, Elisha, and John Strugnell. *Miqṣat Maʿaśe ha-Tôrâh*. DJD 10. Oxford: Clarendon, 1994.

Talmon, Shemaryahu. "Was the Book of Esther Known at Qumran?" *DSD* 2 (1995) 249-67.

Tov, Emanuel. "The Biblical Texts from the Judaean Desert — An Overview and Analysis of the Published Texts." In *The Bible as Book — The Hebrew Bible and the Judaean Desert Discoveries*, ed. E. D. Herbert and E. Tov, 139-66. London: British Library and Oak Knoll Press, 2002.

————. "Groups of Biblical Texts Found at Qumran." In *Time To Prepare the Way in the Wilderness*, ed. Devorah Dimant and Lawrence Schiffman, 85-102. STDJ 16. Leiden: Brill, 1995.

————. "The Orthography and Language of the Hebrew Scrolls Found at Qumran and the Origin of These Scrolls." *Textus* 13 (1986) 31-57.

————. "Rewritten Bible Compositions and Biblical Manuscripts, with Special Attention to the Samaritan Pentateuch." *DSD* 5 (1998) 334-54.

————. "Scriptures: Texts." In *EDSS*, 2:832-36.

Ulrich, Eugene. "Canon." In *EDSS*, 1:117-20.

―――. *The Dead Sea Scrolls and the Origins of the Bible*. SDSSRL. Grand Rapids: Wm. B. Eerdmans, 1999.

VanderKam, James C. *The Dead Sea Scrolls Today*. Grand Rapids: Wm. B. Eerdmans, 1994.

―――, and Peter Flint. *The Meaning of the Dead Sea Scrolls*. San Francisco: HarperSanFrancisco, 2002.

Vermes, Geza. "Bible Interpretation at Qumran." *ErIsr* 20 (1989) 184-91.

―――. *Scripture and Tradition in Judaism*. StPB 4. Leiden: Brill, 1961.

CHAPTER 2

The Text of the Pentateuch at Qumran

At one end of our spectrum of texts lie those texts or books generally accepted across the various groups or communities in Second Temple Judaism as Scripture, that is, a sacred, authoritative text. By the late Second Temple period, when the Qumran community came into existence,[1] we can say with certainty that the Five Books of Moses, the Torah or Pentateuch, were accepted in both the Jewish and Samaritan communities as binding, authoritative Scripture. Further, in the Jewish community, we are fairly sure that all the books now found in the division *Nevi'im*, or Prophets, were considered Scripture. Finally, at least some of the books in the division *Ketubim*, or Writings, were accepted as Scripture (e.g., Psalms, Proverbs, Job). However, the status of certain books that later became canonical is undetermined in this period. Esther, as stated in the Introduction, was almost certainly not considered Scripture by the Qumran community; other books with an uncertain status include Ecclesiastes and Song of Songs. Since this book's focus is on Rewritten Scripture works that use as (one of) their base text(s) a book or books of the Torah or Pentateuch, in this chapter we will investigate the textual characteristics of those books in their base form: Genesis, Exodus, Leviticus, Numbers, and Deuteronomy.

---

1. I accept Magness's reconstruction of the archaeological evidence (based on de Vaux), which places the earliest Second Temple occupation of the site of Qumran around 100 B.C.E. and its destruction at the hands of the Romans in 68 C.E.; Magness, *The Archaeology of Qumran and the Dead Sea Scrolls*, 47-72.

Description of the Evidence

The discoveries in the Judaean Desert caves have given us a window into the textual history of those books that became the Hebrew Bible that was unimaginable 60 years ago. According to Tov,[2] at least two hundred manuscripts of books that later became part of the Hebrew Bible were found in the 11 caves of Qumran. All books in the Hebrew Bible are represented, with the exceptions of Esther and Nehemiah.[3] The oldest scriptural manuscripts are 4QExod-Lev^f and 4QSam^b, dated by Frank Moore Cross to the mid-third century B.C.E.[4] The latest date to the latter half of the first century C.E., around the time of Qumran's destruction at the hands of the Romans in 68 C.E. Thus, we have in the Qumran collection of scriptural scrolls a snapshot of the kind of scriptural texts circulating in the last three hundred years of the Second Temple period.

As we enter into this discussion of textual characteristics in the books of the Torah, it is important to remember that no two manuscripts of any book in antiquity ever looked exactly alike. There are always differences in spelling, inadvertent errors, or minor variations in, for example, proper names that occurred. When we talk about textual characteristics, however, we refer to something more deliberate. According to Eugene Ulrich's definition, we can speak about a "text-type" when we can isolate a relatively large set of manuscripts that display general agreement in certain specific characteristics, against other manuscripts that do not share those characteristics. We may describe these manuscripts as "affiliated."[5] Each biblical book has one or more describable text-types. Sometimes the differences in text-type may be substantial enough to say that two parallel literary editions of the same book circulated in antiquity.[6] A second literary edition exists only if the systematic changes of a definite character are traceable through the entire book. Therefore a book may have two text-types, but not exist in two literary editions.

2. Tov, *Textual Criticism of the Hebrew Bible*, 114-15.

3. The absence of Nehemiah is most likely accidental, since we have fragments of Ezra, and Ezra/Nehemiah was usually considered one book in antiquity. The absence of Esther is, however, probably deliberate; it is evident that the Qumran community did not celebrate the festival of Purim, and the absence of religion in Esther would have made the book unpalatable to them.

4. Cross, *The Ancient Library of Qumran*, 43.

5. Ulrich, *The Dead Sea Scrolls and the Origins of the Bible*, 95. A similar definition is given by Davila, taken from the terminology of New Testament textual criticism: "a text-type is the largest group of sources that can be objectively identified"; "Text-Type and Terminology," 5.

6. Ulrich, *The Dead Sea Scrolls and the Origins of the Bible*, 107.

In the Torah, we have five separate books, with five different textual histories. The text of Leviticus by the late Second Temple period is stable, with no major differences among the various witnesses.[7] The text of Genesis exists in two[8] or three[9] text-types. However, none of the differences are systematic enough to posit a second (or third) literary edition for the entire book. Therefore, a scribe who was working with Genesis or Leviticus as a base text in the creation of a rewritten scriptural text did not have to begin by choosing between different literary editions, although his base text would certainly have contained what we would term variants, depending on the text-type of the manuscript with which he was working. The base text was a relatively solid entity with which to work.

The same is not true for the remaining three books, Exodus, Numbers, and Deuteronomy. Exodus and Numbers have a similar textual history. The books of Exodus and Numbers circulated in two literary editions in antiquity, and copies of both editions were recovered at Qumran. The second version was an intentionally expanded version of the first, primarily through the technique of harmonization. The most complete witnesses to the short version of the text of Exodus are the Masoretic Text and the Septuagint, while the most complete witness to the expanded version of Exodus is the Samaritan Pentateuch. In Numbers, the most complete witness to its short version is the Masoretic Text, while the Samaritan Pentateuch serves as the most complete witness to its expanded version. The three texts just mentioned, the Masoretic Text (MT), the Septuagint (LXX), and the Samaritan Pentateuch (SP), serve as the most complete witnesses to the ancient editions of Exodus and Numbers because they were carefully preserved within three different faith communities. The Masoretic Text is the accepted canonical text of the Jewish community. The Septuagint, a translation of the various books of Jewish Scripture into Greek, done at different times by different translators, became by the third century c.e. the canonical text of the Christians.[10] The Samaritan Pentateuch is, as its name suggests, the canonical text of the Samaritan community. For the purposes of this study, we are chiefly interested in the expanded text-type of the Samaritan Pentateuch.

---

7. Ulrich, *The Dead Sea Scrolls and the Origins of the Bible*, 25; Tov, "The Significance of the Texts from the Judean Desert," 302-3.

8. Davila, "Text-Type and Terminology," 36.

9. Hendel, *The Text of Genesis 1–11*, 79.

10. For a discussion of the history of the Septuagint, see Peters, "Septuagint."

The Samaritan Pentateuch and Harmonization

The Samaritan Pentateuch did not come to the attention of scholars until the 17th century. After its discovery, it was often characterized as a "vulgar" text with a "sectarian" character, and therefore inferior to the Masoretic Text for the purposes of textual criticism.[11] The discovery of the Qumran Scrolls changed scholars' perception of the Samaritan Pentateuch. Several of the manuscripts of Exodus and Numbers found in the caves of Qumran demonstrated that the Samaritan Pentateuch in fact contains an ancient edition of the Pentateuch, current in Palestine in the Second Temple period (hence Cross's preferred sobriquet "Old Palestinian"[12]). The Samaritans adopted this Palestinian text as their canonical text and in the process added to it a thin veneer of sectarian editing, bringing the text into line with their theology. This sectarian editing is easy to isolate. The Samaritans introduced two major changes into the text. First, wherever Jerusalem is alluded to as the central place of worship for the Israelites, the Samaritans inserted a reference to Mount Gerizim (הרגריזים; one word) as God's actual chosen place. This is most evident in the Decalogue in Exodus and Deuteronomy by the addition of a commandment to build an altar on Mount Gerizim: "And when you cross the Jordan you will erect these stone tablets which I am commanding you on Mount Gerizim. And you will build there an altar to the LORD your God, a stone altar" (Exod 20:14b, SP). Second, to emphasize the notion that God had already chosen Mount Gerizim as the appropriate place of worship before the entrance into Canaan, the Samaritan Pentateuch consistently changes the Deuteronomy formula "the place which the LORD <u>will choose</u> (יבחר)," an oblique reference to Jerusalem, to "the place which the LORD <u>has chosen</u> (בחר)," a reference to Mount Gerizim.[13] However, once this thin veneer of sectarian changes is removed (a fairly easy task), what remains is an expanded text of the Pentateuch, characterized by massive and deliberate harmonizations and content editing. This text-type is found at Qumran in several examples, and because of

---

11. Waltke, "Samaritan Pentateuch," 932. Textual criticism is a branch of biblical studies that deals with the forms of the primary text. Text critics both collect data about the similarities and differences among the various ancient witnesses to the text of the Hebrew Bible and attempt to evaluate that data. Although text critics differ about the ultimate goal of their discipline (for one view, see Tov, *Textual Criticism of the Hebrew Bible*, 287-90; for another, see Hendel, *The Text of Genesis 1–11*, 3-5), all agree that the exercise is imperative for establishing the text of the Hebrew Bible.

12. Cross, *The Ancient Library of Qumran*, 139, n. 2.

13. Tov, *Textual Criticism of the Hebrew Bible*, 94-95.

its relation to the Samaritan Pentateuch is called the pre-Samaritan or proto-Samaritan text. Among the scriptural manuscripts from Qumran it is exemplified in its most complete form in the manuscripts 4QpaleoExod^m and 4QNum^b.

A scribe is motivated to harmonize a text when he perceives differences between two parallel texts. These parallel texts may describe the same incident or promulgate the same (or similar) legal ruling. The act of harmonization is meant to smooth out these perceived differences, using two main techniques. The first introduces details found in one text into another, where those details are missing. This may be thought of as taking elements from a "richer" text and importing them into a "poorer" text.[14] The second technique changes the text to avoid any differences between the parallel texts. The scribe does not, however, introduce any element in one text that is not present in another. One scriptural text is used to enhance another.[15] The motivating force behind the act of harmonization is the notion that the text of Scripture is perfect and perfectly harmonious.[16] Thus, all perceived differences should be altered or removed, to achieve the ideal perfection.

The Harmonized Texts of Exodus and Numbers

In the Pentateuch, most harmonizations of the first type occur when elements from Deuteronomy, especially Deuteronomy 1–9, are introduced into the parallel texts in Exodus and Numbers. This makes sense, since Deuteronomy is cast as the speech of Moses to the Israelites on the Plains of Moab prior to their entry into Canaan. To an ancient scribal exegete who takes a harmonizing approach to the text of Scripture, the events Moses rehearses in his speech should agree in detail with those events as narrated in Exodus and Numbers. If they do not, then the two accounts need to be brought into agreement, or harmonized.

One example of this type of harmonization comes from 4Qpaleo-Exod^m. In this harmonization, the story of Jethro's advice to Moses on the selection of judges (Exod 18:13-24, cols. XVIII-XIX) is expanded by Moses' parallel account of the event in Deut 1:9-18. The texts are laid out below, the Exodus account as found in MT on the left, the MT Deuteronomy passage on the right in italics, and the proto-Samaritan harmonized version as found in

---

14. Eshel and Eshel, "Dating the Samaritan Pentateuch's Compilation," 218.
15. Tigay, "Conflation as a Redactional Technique," 62, n. 25.
16. Kugel, "Ancient Biblical Interpretation and the Biblical Sage," 18-19.

4QpaleoExod^m in the middle.[17] The scribal changes made to remove any roughness in the harmonization are underlined.

MT Exod 18:21-27	SP Exod 18:21-27	MT Deut 1:9-18
"You shall seek out for yourself from among all the people capable men who fear God, trustworthy men who spurn ill-gotten gain; and set these over them as chiefs of thousands, chiefs of hundreds, chiefs of fifties and chiefs of tens. Let them exercise authority over the people at all times; let them bring every major matter to you, but decide every minor matter themselves. Make it easier for yourself, and let them share the burden with you. If you do this — and God so commands you — you will be able to bear up; and all these people will go home content." Moses heeded his father-in-law and did all that he had said.	"You shall seek out for yourself from among all the people capable men who fear God, trustworthy men who spurn ill-gotten gain; and set these over them as chiefs of thousands, chiefs of hundreds, chiefs of fifties and chiefs of tens. Let them exercise authority over the people at all times; let them bring every major matter to you, but decide every minor matter themselves. Make it easier for yourself, and let them share the burden with you. If you do this — and God so commands you — you will be able to bear up; and all these people will go home content." Moses heeded his father-in-law and did all that he had said. *Moses said to the people,* "*I myself cannot bear the burden of you alone. The* LORD *your God has multiplied you until you are today as numerous as the stars in the sky. May the* LORD*, the God of your fathers, increase your numbers a thousand-fold, and bless you as He promised you. How can I alone bear the trouble of you, and the burden, and*	*I said to you at that time,* "*I cannot bear the burden of you alone. The* LORD *your God has multiplied you until you are today as numerous as the stars in the sky. May the* LORD*, the God of your fathers, increase your numbers a thousand-fold, and bless you as He promised you. How can I alone bear the trouble of you, and the burden, and*

17. The layout of these texts and much of the following analysis depends heavily on Tigay, "Conflation as a Redactional Technique," 63-68.

MT Exod 18:21-27	SP Exod 18:21-27	MT Deut 1:9-18
	the bickering! Pick from each of your tribes men who are wise, discerning, and experienced, and I will appoint them as your heads." They answered and said, "What you propose to do is good." So he	*the bickering! Pick from each of your tribes men who are wise, discerning, and experienced, and I will appoint them as your heads." You answered me and said, "What you propose to do is good." So I*
Moses chose capable men out of all Israel, and appointed them heads over the people: chiefs of thousands, chiefs of hundreds, chiefs of fifties, and chiefs of tens.	*took their tribal leaders, wise and experienced men, and he appointed them heads over them:* chiefs of thousands, chiefs of hundreds, chiefs of fifties, and chiefs of tens, and officials for their tribes. He charged their magistrates as follows: "Hear out your fellow men, and decide justly between any man and a fellow Israelite or a stranger. You shall not be partial in judgment; hear out high and low alike. Fear no man, for judgment is God's. And any matter that is too difficult for you, you shall bring near to me and I will hear it." Thus he commanded them about the various things that they should do.*	took your tribal leaders, wise and experienced men, and I appointed them heads over you: chiefs of thousands, chiefs of hundreds, chiefs of fifties, and chiefs of tens, and officials for your tribes. I charged your magistrates at that time as follows: "Hear out your fellow men, and decide justly between any man and a fellow Israelite or a stranger. You shall not be partial in judgment; hear out high and low alike. Fear no man, for judgment is God's. And any matter that is too difficult for you, you shall bring near to me and I will hear it." Thus I commanded you at that time about the various things that you should do.*
And they exercised authority over the people at all times: the difficult matters they would bring to Moses, and all the minor matters they would decide themselves. Then Moses bade his father-in-law farewell, and he went his way to his own land.	And they would exercise authority over the people at all times: the major matters they would bring to Moses, and all the minor matters they would decide themselves. Then Moses bade his father-in-law farewell, and he went his way to his own land.	

The major difference between the two accounts that troubled the scribe[18] is that in the Exodus account Jethro advises Moses on how to alleviate his burden of judging and Moses follows his advice, while in Deuteronomy the solution originates with Moses himself and Jethro does not appear. The scribe accomplishes his harmonization in a straightforward manner; he begins with his Exodus text, in which Jethro gives Moses his advice; at the end of v. 24, which states that Moses heeded the advice, he interpolates the Deuteronomy passage, now presented as Moses' speech explaining to the people what he plans to do (on the basis of Jethro's advice above). He excises v. 25 in Exodus as redundant, since the Deuteronomy passage repeats the same information. At the end of the Deuteronomy interpolation, he resumes his Exodus text at v. 26. To ensure a smooth transition between the third person narrative of Exodus and the first person speech of Deuteronomy, he changes some of the first person verbs and pronouns of the Deuteronomy passage to third person. The resulting expanded narrative is very well made; the casual reader would not detect that the interpolation had taken place. This is a classic harmonization, and typical of the narrative portions of the pre-Samaritan text.

A second type of harmonization, changes to avoid differences between parallel texts, occurs in 4QpaleoExod[m] in the plague narratives (Exodus 7–11).[19] The structure of the plague narratives is formulaic: The LORD commands Moses (and Aaron) to perform an act before Pharaoh, Moses (and Aaron) carry out the act, but the magicians of Egypt mimic the act, so Pharaoh's heart is hardened and he refuses to allow the Israelites to leave Egypt.

However, not every pericope of the plague accounts in the version preserved in MT and LXX follows that pattern exactly. Often the execution of the command does not match the words of the command exactly, or it leaves out part of the preceding narrative, so that the text does not make it absolutely explicit that Moses did exactly as the LORD commanded. An example occurs in the plague of blood (Exod 7:14-24).

> Then the LORD said to Moses, "Pharaoh's heart is hardened; he refuses to let the people go. Go to Pharaoh in the morning, as he is going out to the water; stand by at the riverbank to meet him, and take in your hand the staff that was turned into a snake. Say to him, 'The LORD, the God of the Hebrews, sent me to you to say, "Let my people go, so that they may worship me in the wilderness." But until now you have not lis-

18. Although I refer to "the scribe" in the singular, this phenomenon is a scribal tradition, and it is impossible to say now whether or not these harmonizations took place all at one time or were the work of one scribe.

19. Sanderson, *An Exodus Scroll from Qumran*, 196-206.

tened. Thus says the LORD, "By this you shall know that I am the LORD."
See, with the staff that is in my hand I will strike the water that is in the
Nile, and it shall be turned to blood. The fish in the river shall die, the
river itself shall stink, and the Egyptians shall be unable to drink water
from the Nile.'" The LORD said to Moses, "Say to Aaron, 'Take your staff
and stretch out your hand over the waters of Egypt — over its rivers, its
canals, and its ponds, and all its pools of water — so that they may become blood; and there shall be blood throughout the whole land of
Egypt, even in vessels of wood and in vessels of stone.'" Moses and
Aaron did just as the LORD commanded. In the sight of Pharaoh and of
his officials he lifted up the staff and struck the water in the river, and
all the water in the river was turned into blood, and the fish in the river
died. The river stank so that the Egyptians could not drink its water,
and there was blood throughout the whole land of Egypt. But the magicians of Egypt did the same by their secret arts; so Pharaoh's heart re-
mained hardened, and he would not listen to them; as the LORD had
said. Pharaoh turned and went into his house, and he did not take even
this to heart. And all the Egyptians had to dig along the Nile for water
to drink, for they could not drink the water of the river.

Notice that when Moses executes the command he does not repeat the instruction to Aaron that the LORD has just told Moses to give, although it is
implied in the sentence "Moses and Aaron did just as the LORD commanded."

This omission did not accord with the scribe's vision of the absolute
harmony of the text: the command and its fulfillment should use exactly the
same words as had been spoken by the LORD. Thus, in the pre-Samaritan text
the plague of blood reads as follows (the harmonization is marked by italics):

Then the LORD said to Moses, "Pharaoh's heart is hardened; he refuses to
let the people go. Go to Pharaoh in the morning, as he is going out to the
water; stand by at the riverbank to meet him, and take in your hand the
staff that was turned into a snake. Say to him, 'The LORD, the God of the
Hebrews, sent me to you to say, "Let my people go, so that they may worship me in the wilderness." But until now you have not listened. Thus says
the LORD, "By this you shall know that I am the LORD." See, with the staff
that is in my hand I will strike the water that is in the Nile, and it shall be
turned to blood. The fish in the river shall die, the river itself shall stink,
and the Egyptians shall be unable to drink water from the Nile.'" *So Moses
and Aaron went to Pharaoh and said to him, "The LORD, the God of the Hebrews, has sent us to you saying, 'Let my people go so that they might serve
me in the wilderness,' and behold, you have not listened until now. Therefore*

thus says the LORD, *'By this you will know that I am the* LORD*.' Behold, with the staff that is in my hand I am striking the water that is in the Nile, and it shall be turned to blood. The fish in the river shall die, the river itself shall stink, and the Egyptians shall be unable to drink water from the Nile."* And the LORD said to Moses, "Say to Aaron, 'Take your staff and stretch out your hand over the waters of Egypt . . .'" (SP Exod 7:14-19a)

The scribe has inserted the LORD's speech to Moses giving him the command into Moses' speech to Pharaoh, executing the command. Thus the command and execution are carried out with exactly the same words, yielding a highly repetitive text.

In other places in the plague stories the command is lacking; only the execution is narrated, as in the plague of locusts (Exod 10:1-6, 12-15):

Then the LORD said to Moses, "Go to Pharaoh; for I have hardened his heart and the heart of his officials, in order that I may show these signs of mine among them, and that you may tell your children and grandchildren how I have made fools of the Egyptians and what signs I have done among them — so that you may know that I am the LORD." So Moses and Aaron went to Pharaoh, and said to him, "Thus says the LORD, the God of the Hebrews, 'How long will you refuse to humble yourself before me? Let my people go, so that they may worship me. For if you refuse to let my people go, tomorrow I will bring locusts into your country. They shall cover the surface of the land, so that no one will be able to see the land. They shall devour the last remnant left you after the hail, and they shall devour every tree of yours that grows in the field. They shall fill your houses, and the houses of all your officials and of all the Egyptians — something that neither your parents nor your grandparents have seen, from the day they came on earth to this day.'" Then he turned and went out from Pharaoh. . . . Then the LORD said to Moses, "Stretch out your hand over the land of Egypt, so that the locusts may come upon it and eat every plant in the land, all that the hail has left." So Moses stretched out his staff over the land of Egypt, and the LORD brought an east wind upon the land all that day and all that night; when morning came, the east wind had brought the locusts. The locusts came upon all the land of Egypt and settled on the whole country of Egypt, such a dense swarm of locusts as had never been before, nor ever shall be again. They covered the surface of the whole land, so that the land was black; and they ate all the plants in the land and all the fruit of the trees that the hail had left; nothing green was left, no tree, no plant in the field, in all the land of Egypt.

What is missing in this passage is the LORD's command to Moses before he and Aaron go to Pharaoh. Again, this absence signaled to the scribe the need for a harmonizing expansion:

> Then the LORD said to Moses, "Go to Pharaoh; for I have hardened his heart and the heart of his officials, in order that I may show these signs of mine among them, and that you may tell your children and grandchildren how I have made fools of the Egyptians and what signs I have done among them — so that you may know that I am the LORD *your God." And you will say to Pharaoh, "Thus says the LORD, the God of the Hebrews, 'How long will you refuse to humble yourself before me? Let my people go, so that they may worship me. For if you refuse to let my people go, tomorrow I will bring locusts into your country. They shall cover the surface of the land, so that no one will be able to see the land. They shall devour the last remnant left you after the hail, and they shall devour every tree of yours that grows in the field. They shall fill your houses, and the houses of all your officials and of all the Egyptians — something that neither your parents nor your grandparents have seen from the day they came on earth to this day.'"* So Moses and Aaron went to Pharaoh, and said to him, "Thus says the LORD, the God of the Hebrews, 'How long will you refuse to humble yourself before me? Let my people go, so that they may worship me. For if you refuse to let my people go, tomorrow I will bring locusts into your country. They shall cover the surface of the land, so that no one will be able to see the land. They shall devour the last remnant left you after the hail, and they shall devour every tree of yours that grows in the field. They shall fill your houses, and the houses of all your officials and of all the Egyptians — something that neither your parents nor your grandparents have seen from the day they came on earth to this day.'" Then he turned and went out from Pharaoh. . . .

The scribe has added the missing command of the LORD to Moses before Moses and Aaron go to Pharaoh, by replicating Moses' speech to Pharaoh, which he delivers as a command of the LORD. Once again this yields a highly repetitive text, but one that leaves nothing to the imagination of the reader. Commands and their fulfillment are carried out exactly. Any possible hint of inconsistency in the scriptural text, unthinkable in this approach to the text, is thus eliminated, and a harmonized narrative is the result.

The book of Numbers in the pre-Samaritan tradition exhibits the same type of harmonizations, as evidenced in the manuscript 4QNum[b].[20] Thus we

20. Jastram, "4QNum[b]." The following harmonizations in the book of Numbers are pre-

29

have at Qumran two complete, although fragmentary, examples of texts of Scripture in the pre-Samaritan tradition.

The Harmonized Text of Deuteronomy

We have noted that in the late Second Temple period two variant literary editions of Exodus and Numbers were in circulation, and both are preserved at Qumran: the proto-rabbinic text-type and the pre-Samaritan text-type. For Deuteronomy the situation is slightly different. There is no evidence from antiquity that more than one literary edition of the complete book of Deuteronomy was ever in circulation. However, there is a great deal of evidence that shows that passages from Deuteronomy were subject to harmonistic editing. These passages are especially prominent in manuscripts in which Deuteronomy pericopes, by themselves or with pericopes from other books, are excerpted for liturgical or study purposes.[21] The same techniques of harmonization that we observed in the pre-Samaritan texts of Exodus and Numbers are evident in these manuscripts, indicating that the phenomenon was a widespread, legitimate scribal technique when working with the texts of Scripture. We will look at three examples: 4QDeut[n], the Nash Papyrus, and 4QPhyl G.

4QDeut[n], an exquisite, well-preserved small manuscript from Cave 4, Qumran, contains four complete and two partially damaged columns. Column 1 contains only Deut 8:5-10, while cols. 2-6 contain Deut 5:1–6:1 as a running text.[22] Since this was the order of the columns in antiquity, and since it is unlikely that the manuscript, for reasons of size, ever contained the entire book of Deuteronomy, 4QDeut[n] has been identified as a manuscript of excerpted texts made for study or liturgical purposes. How exactly the manuscript functioned in antiquity is unclear. It has been suggested that it contained the texts for various prayers taken from Deuteronomy, since in the rabbinic tradition Deut 8:5-10 is the scriptural basis for the duty of blessing after meals[23] and Deut 5:1–6:1 is used as a prayer text in the Qumran phylacteries.

4QDeut[n] is classified as a harmonized text in the pre-Samaritan tradition[24] because in its text of the Decalogue a scribe has imported ele-

---

served in 4QNum[b]: following 20:13; 21:12; 21:13; 21:21; 27:23. Jastram also reconstructs harmonizations after 12:16; 21:22; 21:23; and 31:21. These reconstructions agree with the SP (Jastram, 215).

21. Duncan, "Deuteronomy, Book of," 201.
22. Crawford, "4QDeut[n]," 117.
23. Weinfeld, "Grace after Meals in Qumran."
24. Eshel, "4QDeut[n]."

ments from the Exodus version of the Decalogue, in particular in the Sabbath commandment. This is the reverse of the harmonizing direction that we observed in the pre-Samaritan tradition of Exodus and Numbers and demonstrates that harmonizations could occur from an earlier (in order, not date) book into a later one. The harmonization in 4QDeut[n] is routine, with the scribal intervention perhaps more clearly marked than we have previously seen. The text is laid out below. MT Deuteronomy is on the left, MT Exodus is on the right in italics, and 4QDeut[n] is in the center, with the scribal changes underlined.[25]

MT Deut 5:12-15	4QDeut[n] 5:12-15	MT Exod 20:8-11
Observe the Sabbath day to sanctify it, according as the LORD your God has commanded you. Six days you shall labor and do all your work, but the seventh day is a Sabbath to the LORD your God; you shall not do any work, you, or your son or your daughter, or your manservant or your maidservant, or your ox or your ass or any of your cattle, or your stranger who is in your gates, in order that your manservant and your maidservant might rest like you. And you will remember that you were a servant in the land of Egypt, and the LORD your God brought you forth from there with a mighty hand and an outstretched arm; therefore the LORD your God commanded you to keep the Sabbath day.	Observe the Sabbath day to sanctify it, according as the LORD your God has commanded you. Six days you shall labor and do all your work, but <u>on</u> the seventh day is a Sabbath to the LORD your God; you shall not do <u>in it</u> any work, you, your son, your daughter, your manservant or your maidservant, your ox or your ass or your cattle, your stranger who is in your gates, in order that your manservant and your maidservant might rest like you. And you will remember that you were a servant in the land of Egypt, and the LORD your God brought you forth from there with a mighty hand and an outstretched arm; therefore the LORD your God commanded you to <u>observe</u> the Sabbath day	*Remember the Sabbath day to sanctify it.* *Six days* *you shall labor and do* *all your work, but the* *seventh day is a Sab-* *bath to the LORD your* *God; you shall not do* *any work, you, or* *your son or your daughter,* *your manservant* *or your maidservant,* *or your cattle,* *or your stranger who* *is in your gates.*

25. The textual variants among the various versions of the Decalogue are much more complicated than can be demonstrated here. I have not noted the "inner" variants that are not the result of harmonization. The interested reader is referred to Crawford, "4QDeut[n]," 124-26.

MT Deut 5:12-15	4QDeut[n] 5:12-15	MT Exod 20:8-11
	to sanctify it. *For six days*	*For six days*
	the LORD made the hea-	*the LORD made the hea-*
	vens and the earth,	*vens and the earth,*
	the sea and all that is	*the sea and all that is*
	in them, and he rested	*in them, and he rested*
	on the seventh day.	*on the seventh day.*
	Therefore the LORD	*Therefore the LORD*
	blessed the day of the	*blessed the day of the*
	Sabbath to sanctify it.	*Sabbath and he sanctified it.*

The scribe's activity is transparent. Recognizing that the versions of the Decalogue in Deuteronomy and Exodus give very different reasons for Sabbath observance, he has combined them. Since his main or base text is Deuteronomy, he has interpolated the Exodus justification after the complete text of the Deuteronomy commandment, using the phrase "to sanctify it" (לקדשו) as a noticeable seam. The result is a very long commandment, but one that would put to rest any concerns about the differences between Deuteronomy and Exodus.

The second example of a small liturgical text that shows evidence of harmonization is not a Qumran document, but was discovered in Egypt, indicating that the practice of harmonization was widespread, even beyond the borders of Palestine. The Nash Papyrus is a mid-second century B.C.E. papyrus document, in Hebrew, discovered somewhere in the Fayyum of Egypt.[26] The papyrus contains the Decalogue and the Shema (Deut 6:4-5), both texts that were part of Jewish liturgy at least from the Second Temple period onward. The Nash Papyrus is therefore most likely a liturgical text. Its text is harmonized, but not in a systematic or even perhaps a deliberate fashion; rather, the separate versions of Exodus and Deuteronomy cross-fertilized each other to produce a hybrid text. It is possible that the scribe was copying from memory and the harmonizations were inadvertent. In any case, the text of the Nash Papyrus indicates the textual fluidity, and the tendency toward expansion, common in scriptural texts in the late Second Temple period.

As an illustration of the hybrid nature of the Nash Papyrus, here is its version of the fourth commandment of the Decalogue. Although there is some disagreement about the scribe's base text,[27] in the fourth commandment the base text seems to be Exodus, with insertions from Deuteronomy. The (MT) Deuteronomy insertions are indicated by italics; other changes,

---

26. Cook, "A Pre-Massoretic Biblical Papyrus"; Albright, "A Biblical Fragment from the Maccabaean Age."

27. See Eshel, "4QDeut[n]," 123, n. 36.

which may be the result of the scribe's different text tradition, are underlined.[28] Brackets indicate where the papyrus is broken.

> Remember the Sabbath day, to [sanctify it. Six day]s you shall labor and
> do all your work, but <u>on</u> the [seventh] day [is a Sabbath to the LORD] your
> God. You will not do <u>in it</u> any work, [you, or your son or your daughter,]
> your manservant or your maidservant, *your ox or your ass* or *any of* [your]
> cat[tle, or your stranger who] is in your gates. For six days the L[ORD]
> made [the heaven]s and the earth, the sea and all th[at is in them; and he
> rested on the] seventh[day.] Therefore the LORD blessed the <u>seventh</u>
> [day,] and he sanctified it.

The harmonizations are minor, and, as suggested above, may not even be deliberate. What the papyrus does demonstrate, however, is how the scribe's
command of the text, and his awareness of the differences between parallel
passages in his received text (in this case close to the version preserved in MT/
LXX), led to the type of expansions typical of the pre-Samaritan family of
texts.

The next example of a harmonized text is certainly a text for liturgical
use, for it is from one of the numerous phylacteries or tefillin found in the
Qumran caves.[29] Twenty-two phylacteries were found in the Qumran caves,
indicating that the use of tefillin had been established in Palestine by the late
Second Temple period. By the rabbinic period the passages to be included in
the tefillin had been standardized to four: Exod 13:1-10; 13:11-16; Deut 6:4-9;
and 11:13-21. The Qumran tefillin, however, contain a wider array of passages
beyond those mandated by the rabbis, including Deut 5:1–6:9; 10:12–11:21;
Exod 12:43–13:16; and, in one case, Deuteronomy 32. This wider array of texts
indicates that the selection of passages to be included in tefillin had not stabi-
lized prior to the rabbinic period.[30]

Several of the phylacteries exhibit a harmonized text: 4QPhyl G, J,
8QPhyl, and XQPhyl 3.[31] As we saw with the Nash Papyrus, it is difficult to be

---

28. Notice that some of these changes agree with 4QDeut[n] as given above, as well as with
the LXX version of Exodus. The scribe's base text obviously differed in minor ways from the
MT.

29. "Tefillin" is the Aramaic word for the two small black boxes with leather straps, containing particular passages of Scripture, which observant male Jews wear on the forehead and
left forearm during prayer; "phylactery" is the Greek equivalent of this word.

30. The selection of these passages is in no way sectarian, as argued by Schiffman, "Phylacteries and Mezuzot," 676, but simply indicates a wider latitude of practice among Jews in the
late Second Temple period.

31. Eshel and Eshel, "Dating the Samaritan Pentateuch's Compilation," 228.

certain whether these harmonizations were deliberate (as was certainly the case with 4QDeut[n]) or the unconscious result of the scribe's knowledge of the parallel texts.[32] In any case, it is clear that these harmonized texts were considered valid Scripture passages, since they were used in phylacteries.

As an example we will use the fourth commandment of the Decalogue as found in 4QPhyl G.[33] This phylactery contains Deut 5:1-21 on the *recto* and Exod 13:11-12 on the *verso*. The governing text of the Decalogue is clearly Deuteronomy, since it begins with Deut 5:1: "And Moses called to all Israel, and said to them, 'Hear, O Israel, the statutes and the commandments that I am <u>commanding you today, concerning the word</u> in your ears <u>this</u> day, and you will observe to do them.'" Even in this short verse there are variants (indicated by underlining) from the MT and the SP. Nevertheless, the text is clearly recognizable as Deuteronomy. However, when we reach the fourth commandment, the scribe (whether deliberately or not we cannot be sure) interpolates the Exodus version of the commandment, with some remnants of Deuteronomy remaining. The text is translated here, with brackets indicating where the parchment is broken. Text from Deuteronomy is indicated by italics, while variants from the major Exodus version are indicated by underlining.

> ?[34] the day of the Sabba]th, to sa[nctify it.] Six days you shall labor and do all your work, but <u>on</u> [the seventh day is a Sabbath to the LORD]D your God {the seventh to the LORD your God}.[35] You shall not [d]o an[y work; yo]u, or your son, or your daughter, <u>the servant of your daughter</u>[36] [or] your [maid]servant, *or your ox or your ass or any of* [your] cat[tle, or your stranger w]ho is in your gates. For six [days] the LORD [made] the [he]avens and the [earth, the se]a and all that is in them, and he rested on [the sevent]h [day.] Therefore the LORD bl[es]sed the [Sa]bbath [day] and [he] sanctified it.

Note that the beginning of the commandment does not contain the characteristic Deuteronomic phrase, "as the LORD your God commanded you." The reason given for Sabbath observance is from Exodus; the Deuteronomic reason is absent. These variations are enough to indicate that this is an Exodus interpolation in the midst of a Deuteronomy text. The scribe's reason for

---

32. Brooke, "Deuteronomy 5–6 in the Phylacteries from Qumran Cave 4," 59.

33. Milik, "Tefillin, Mezuzot et Targums," 58-60.

34. Milik, the editor, did not know whether to restore "remember" (זכור) of Exodus or "observe" (שמור) of Deuteronomy. My instinct would be to restore "remember."

35. This is a case of simple dittography, or inadvertent repetition, a common scribal error.

36. This is most likely another dittography.

changing his base text right here is unclear; a simple lapse of memory cannot be ruled out. After this Exodus interpolation, the scribe returns to his governing Deuteronomy text.

4QTestimonia

The three examples given above (4QDeut[n], the Nash Papyrus, and 4QPhyl G), which demonstrate how passages from Deuteronomy may be subject to expansion and harmonization, are all small texts created for liturgical use. None of them can be labeled "sectarian." That is, they do not display any particular sectarian characteristics of the Essene movement and could have been in use among any Jewish group in the late Second Temple period.[37] Our last example of a harmonized text comes, however, from a document that is without doubt sectarian and most likely a Qumran composition: 4QTestimonia (4Q175). This manuscript, an early first-century C.E. composition in Hebrew, consists of one sheet of text, which collects messianic proof-texts from Exodus, Numbers, Deuteronomy, and the Psalms of Joshua.[38] What is interesting for our purposes is that the composer chose for his Exodus quotation a text in the pre-Samaritan tradition, while his Deuteronomy text contains an expansionistic variant in agreement with the Septuagint and 4QDeut[h], against the other versions.[39] In other words, the scribe chose what we would identify as two different text-types for his anthology of Scripture passages. These textual choices demonstrate that the scribal composer did not discriminate between text-types; evidently all these variant texts were equally authoritative to him.

The first quotation is from Exod 20:18 in the pre-Samaritan version, which interpolates, after v. 18, two pericopes from Deuteronomy concerning the coming "prophet like Moses": Deut 5:28-29 and 18:18-19. 4QTestimonia's text is given on the left, with the parallel text from the Samaritan Pentateuch on the right. Differences between the two texts are underlined.

4QTestimonia, lines 1-8	Exod 20:18b (SP)
And the Lord spoke to Moses, saying, "You have heard the sound of the words of this people, which they spoke to you.	And the Lord spoke to Moses, saying, "I have heard the sound of the words of this people, which they spoke to you.

37. A possible exception to this statement is the circles of priests and scribes associated with the temple; Tov argues that they preserved the proto-rabbinic text of the Pentateuch exclusively; "Textual Criticism of the Hebrew Bible 1947-1997," 64.

38. Allegro, *Qumrân Cave 4.I*, 57-60; see now Parry and Tov, *Exegetical Texts*, 134-37.

39. Duncan, "4QDeut[h]," 68-69.

4QTestimonia, lines 1-8	Exod 20:18b (SP)
All which they have spoken is good. Who will make their heart thus, to fear me and to observe <u>all</u> my commandments all the days, so that it will be good for them and for their children forever? A prophet like you I will raise up for them from the midst of their brethren, and I will put my words in his mouth, and he will speak to them all that I will command him. And anyone who does not listen to <u>my</u> words which <u>the prophet</u> will speak in my name, I myself will seek from his people."	All which they have spoken is good. Who will make their heart thus, to fear me and to observe my commandments all the days, so that it will be good for them and for their children forever? A prophet like you I will raise up for them from the midst of their brethren, and I will put my words in his mouth, and he will speak to them all that I will command him. And anyone who does not listen to <u>his</u> words which <u>he</u> will speak in my name, I myself will seek from his people."

The two texts are almost identical, because they are both copies from a pre-Samaritan expanded text of Exodus.

The quotation from Deuteronomy, however, is not from the pre-Samaritan tradition, but contains an expansion that is also contained in another Qumran manuscript, 4QDeut[h], as well as the Septuagint.[40] A portion of the text follows, with the expansion underlined:

> And of Levi he said: "<u>Give to Levi</u> your Thummim, and your Urim to your loyal one, whom you tested at Massah, with whom you contended at the waters of Meribah; who said of his father and mother, I know them not; he ignored his kin, and did not acknowledge his children." (Deut 33:8-9a)

The added phrase "Give to Levi" yields a smoother text, but the shorter text is probably correct; the expansion is a scribal gloss to "improve" (according to this scribal tradition) the text. By choosing two text-types for his quotations, the scribe of the Testimonia gives us an example of the freedom that scribal redactors/composers in this period had in choosing the scriptural texts with which they worked.

Conclusion

The evidence from Qumran demonstrates that during the Second Temple period there were different approaches to the transmission of the scriptural text. In particular, one scribal tradition approached the text with the understanding that the biblical text was harmonious and perfect; if there were perceived

---

40. In fact, Tov suggests that the 4QTestimonia scribe copied his Deuteronomy quotation from 4QDeut[h]; "Groups of Biblical Texts Found at Qumran," 85.

imperfections, they should be removed by scribal intervention into the text. In addition, most groups within the broad parameters of Judaism at this time did not insist upon a single textual tradition, but were willing to accept a certain amount of textual flux,[41] even to the point of accepting two parallel literary editions of the same text as valid Scripture. Further, the role of the scribe in copying, expanding, and updating the scriptural text was an important one, which the scribes themselves took very seriously. This chapter has demonstrated the work of these scribes as they compared and harmonized or edited the Scriptures they had inherited; our next chapter demonstrates that the creative work of the scribes went beyond "innerscriptural" harmonizing to adding nonscriptural material into their received text.

BIBLIOGRAPHY

Albright, William F. "A Biblical Fragment from the Maccabaean Age: The Nash Papyrus." *JBL* 56 (1937) 145-76.

Allegro, John M. *Qumrân Cave 4.I.* DJD 5. Oxford: Clarendon, 1968.

Brooke, George J. "Deuteronomy 5–6 in the Phylacteries from Qumran Cave 4." In *Emanuel: Studies in Hebrew Bible, Septuagint, and Dead Sea Scrolls in Honor of Emanuel Tov,* ed. Shalom M. Paul, Robert A. Kraft, Lawrence H. Schiffman, and Weston W. Fields, 57-70. VTSup 94. Leiden: Brill, 2003.

Cook, S. A. "A Pre-Massoretic Biblical Papyrus." *Proceedings of the Society of Biblical Archaeology* 25 (1903) 34-56.

Crawford, Sidnie White. "4QDeut^n." In *Qumran Cave 4.IX,* ed. Eugene Ulrich, Frank Moore Cross, *et al.,* 117-28. DJD 14. Oxford: Clarendon, 1994.

Cross, Frank Moore. *The Ancient Library of Qumran.* 3rd ed. Minneapolis: Fortress, 1995.

Davila, James R. "Text-Type and Terminology: Genesis and Exodus as Test Cases." *RevQ* 16 (1993-95) 3-37.

Duncan, Julie Ann. "Deuteronomy, Book of." In *EDSS,* 1:198-202.

———. "4QDeut^h." In *Qumran Cave 4.IX,* ed. Eugene Ulrich, Frank Moore Cross, *et al.,* 61-70. DJD 14. Oxford: Clarendon, 1994.

Eshel, Esther. "4QDeut^n — A Text That Has Undergone Harmonistic Editing." *HUCA* 62 (1991) 117-54.

———, and Hanan Eshel. "Dating the Samaritan Pentateuch's Compilation in Light of the Qumran Biblical Scrolls." In *Emanuel: Studies in Hebrew Bible, Septuagint, and Dead Sea Scrolls in Honor of Emanuel Tov,* ed. Shalom M.

41. Tov, "Textual Criticism of the Hebrew Bible 1947-1997," 64.

Paul, Robert A. Kraft, Lawrence H. Schiffman, and Weston W. Fields, 215-40. VTSup 94. Leiden: Brill, 2003.

Hendel, Ronald S. *The Text of Genesis 1–11*. New York: Oxford University Press, 1998.

Jastram, Nathan. "4QNum^b." In *Qumran Cave 4.VII: Genesis to Numbers,* ed. Eugene Ulrich, Frank Moore Cross, *et al.,* 205-67. DJD 12. Oxford: Clarendon, 1994.

Kugel, James L. "Ancient Biblical Interpretation and the Biblical Sage." In *Studies in Ancient Midrash*, 1-26. Cambridge, MA: Harvard University Press, 2001.

Magness, Jodi. *The Archaeology of Qumran and the Dead Sea Scrolls.* SDSSRL. Grand Rapids: Wm. B. Eerdmans, 2002.

Milik, J. T. "Tefillin, Mezuzot et Targums." In *Qumrân Grotte 4.II*, ed. Roland de Vaux and Milik, 31-91. DJD 6. Oxford: Clarendon, 1977.

Parry, Donald W., and Emanuel Tov. *Exegetical Texts.* The Dead Sea Scrolls Reader, Pt. 2. Leiden: Brill, 2004.

Peters, Melvin K. H. "Septuagint." In *ABD,* 5:1093-1104.

Sanderson, Judith E. *An Exodus Scroll from Qumran: 4QpaleoExod^m and the Samaritan Tradition.* HSS 30. Atlanta: Scholars, 1986.

Schiffman, Lawrence H. "Phylacteries and Mezuzot." In *EDSS,* 2:675-77.

Tigay, Jeffrey H. "Conflation as a Redactional Technique." In *Empirical Models for Biblical Criticism,* 53-89. Philadelphia: University of Pennsylvania Press, 1985.

Tov, Emanuel. "Groups of Biblical Texts Found at Qumran." In *Time To Prepare the Way in the Wilderness,* ed. Devorah Dimant and Lawrence Schiffman, 85-102. STDJ 16. Leiden: Brill, 1995.

————. "The Significance of the Texts from the Judean Desert for the History of the Text of the Hebrew Bible: A New Synthesis." In *Qumran between the Old and New Testaments,* ed. Frederick H. Cryer and Thomas L. Thompson, 277-309. JSOTSup 290. Sheffield: Sheffield Academic, 1998.

————. *Textual Criticism of the Hebrew Bible.* 2nd rev. ed. Minneapolis: Fortress and Assen: Royal Van Gorcum, 2001.

————. "Textual Criticism of the Hebrew Bible 1947-1997." In *Perspectives in the Study of the Old Testament and Early Judaism,* ed. Florentino García Martínez and Edward Noort, 61-81. VTSup 73. Leiden: Brill, 1998.

Ulrich, Eugene. *The Dead Sea Scrolls and the Origins of the Bible.* SDSSRL. Grand Rapids: Wm. B. Eerdmans, 1999.

Waltke, Bruce K. "Samaritan Pentateuch." In *ABD,* 5:932-40.

Weinfeld, Moshe. "Grace After Meals in Qumran." *JBL* 111 (1992) 427-40.

CHAPTER 3

Reworked Pentateuch

The next group of manuscripts along the spectrum to be considered is the texts that have been gathered under the rubric "Reworked Pentateuch." These manuscripts demonstrate that the tradition of scribal exegesis discussed in the Introduction and demonstrated by the pre-Samaritan manuscripts continued well into the late Second Temple period. The Reworked Pentateuch manuscripts include 4Q364, 4Q365, 4Q366 and 4Q367.[1] A fifth manuscript, 4Q158, is often grouped along with the other four, although it was originally published independently as "Biblical Paraphrase."[2]

When Emanuel Tov and I first began work on these manuscripts in the early 1990s, and subsequently in the *editio princeps,* we spoke about them in terms of a single "composition" written by an "author," who used a "biblical base text," which he then extensively altered. In the decade since these initial publications, as our knowledge of the state of the text of Scripture in the Second Temple period has grown, such designations are no longer apt and should be rejected (see Introduction). Rather, what we see in this group of texts, which is probably more extensive than the original five, is the next point on our spectrum.[3] These texts are the product of scribal interpreta-

1. Tov and White, "Reworked Pentateuch."
2. Allegro, "Biblical Paraphrase: Genesis, Exodus," 1-6.
3. It has been suggested, for example, that 2QExod[b] and 4QparaGen-Exod belong to this group. By referring to these five texts as a group, I mean that they share enough characteristics, especially in their contents and their method of exegesis, to differentiate them from other types or genres of works. However, their differences indicate that they are not copies of the same composition. I agree here with Brooke, who refers to them as "separate compositions of the same genre"; "4Q158: Reworked Pentateuch[a] or Reworked Pentateuch A?," 241.

tion, still marked mainly by harmonistic editing, but with one important addition: the insertion of outside material into the text, material not found in other parts of what we now recognize as the Pentateuch. This change in scribal procedure raises the question of the authority and function of these texts in the Second Temple period, a question I shall attempt to answer at the end of this chapter. First, let us take a closer look at these texts in order to ascertain their characteristics.

The Reworked Pentateuch Group as Harmonizing Texts

The main exemplars of this category are the manuscripts 4QReworked Pentateuch[b] (4Q364) and 4QReworked Pentateuch[c] (4Q365), because they are the most extensively preserved.[4] Both manuscripts were copied sometime between 75-50 B.C.E., the late Hasmonaean period. Each probably contained a text of what we now call the entire Pentateuch, in the familiar order of Genesis, Exodus, Leviticus (note that 4Q364 does not contain any fragments from Leviticus), Numbers, and Deuteronomy. This is very compelling evidence that by the first century B.C.E. these books were considered a discrete unit of Scripture, although the five books continued to be copied separately as well (see, e.g., 4QDeut[g], which dates from the second half of the first century C.E.).

4Q364 and 4Q365 contain only one small fragment of overlapping text, at Exod 26:33-35 (4Q364, frg. 17; 4Q365, frgs. 8a-b). At this overlap the two manuscripts share a reading against the witnesses of the Masoretic Text and the Samaritan Pentateuch: הארון (with the definite article) vs. ארון (the construct form without the definite article). No firm conclusions can be drawn from this shared reading, but it may point to a common textual tradition.

---

4. 4Q364: Gen 25:18-21; Gen 26:7-8; Gen 27:39 or 41; Gen 28:6; Gen 29:32-3?; Gen 30:1-4; Gen 30:26-36; Gen 31:47-53; Gen 32:18-20; Gen 32:26-30; Gen 34:2; Gen 35:28; Gen 37:7-8; Gen 38:14-21; Gen 44:30–45:1; Gen 45:21-27; Gen 48:14-15; Exod 21:14-22; Exod 24:12-14; Exod 24:18; Exod 25:1-2; Exod 26:1; Exod 26:33-35; Num 14:16-20; Num 20:17-18; Num 33:31-49; Deut 1:1-6; Deut 1:17-33; Deut 1:45-46; Deut 2:8-14; Deut 2:30–3:2; Deut 3:18-23; Deut 9:6-7; Deut 9:12-18; Deut 9:22-24; Deut 9:27-29; Deut 10:1-4; Deut 10:6-7; Deut 10:10-13; Deut 10:22–11:2; Deut 11:6-9; Deut 11:23-24; Deut 14:24-26.

4Q365: Gen 21:9-10; Exod 8:13-19; Exod 9:9-12; Exod 10:19-20; Exod 14:10; Exod 14:12-21; Exod 15:16-20; Exod 15:22-26; Exod 17:3-5; Exod 18:13-16; Exod 26:34-36; Exod 28:16-20; Exod 29:20-22; Exod 30:37–31:2; Exod 35:3-5; Exod 36:32-38; Exod 37:29–38:7; Exod 39:1-16; Exod 29:17-19; Lev 11:1-2; Lev 11:17-24; Lev 11:32; Lev 11:40-45; Lev 13:6-8; Lev 13:15-18; Lev 13:51-52; Lev 16:6-7 or 11-12 or 17-18; Lev 18:26-28; Lev 23:42–24:2; Lev 25:7-9; Lev 26:17-32; Lev 27:34; Num 1:1-5; Num 3:26-30; Num 4:47-49; Num 7:1; Num 7:78-80; Num 8:11-12; Num 9:15–10:3; Num 13:12-25; Num 13:29-30; Num 15:26-28; Num 17:20-24; Num 27:11; Num 36:1-2; Deut 2:24 or 36; Deut 19:20–20:1.

Both 4Q364 and 4Q365 belong in the pre-Samaritan textual tradition that was discussed in the preceding chapter. This tradition has been described as harmonistic or expansive, and we can see those scribal techniques at work in 4Q364 and 4Q365. The most complete exemplar of this group of texts is the Samaritan Pentateuch (prior to its sectarian editing by the Samaritan community); 4Q364 and 4Q365 are often in agreement with the Samaritan Pentateuch against other textual witnesses.[5] However, it is a mistake to claim that 4Q364 or 4Q365 used the pre-Samaritan text as its "base text"; rather, it is more exact to say that both manuscripts come out of the same scribal trajectory and therefore share a common exegetical tradition, which is manifested in the large number of agreements among the texts. However, there are also disagreements, which indicate that these texts are not copies of one another but are part of a tradition in which an individual scribe (or group of scribes) had freedom to manipulate a received text within a broader body of tradition. The manuscripts themselves illustrate this.

4Q364 contains many examples of small exegetical comments, which function as aids to the reader within the narrative flow of the text. The very first preserved fragment gives an example of this phenomenon, in Gen 25:19:

> [And these are the descendants of I]saac, the son of Abraham;[he begat Isaac] *whom Sarah [his] wife b[ore] to him.*

The phrase "whom Sarah his wife bore to him" is not found in any other textual witness to v. 19 and is probably added in the tradition to remind the reader that Isaac is the son of Sarah (unlike Ishmael, the son of Hagar) and therefore the heir to God's promise to Abraham earlier in Genesis. Notice that in Gen 25:12, where the genealogy of Ishmael begins, Ishmael is identified as the son of Hagar and thus by implication as not the heir to the promise. The fact that v. 12 identifies Ishmael's mother may have prompted the identification of Isaac's mother in v. 19 of 4Q634. Whether this was done by the scribe of 4Q364 or earlier in the tradition, we cannot say.

4Q365 contains the same type of short exegetical comment. Frg. 5 contains Exod 14:10:

> [And] they looked, and behold, the Egyptians were coming after the[m, and they feared greatly . . .] . . . . *thousand horses and six hundred [chari]ots . . .*

5. See Tov and White, "Reworked Pentateuch," 193-95. A. Kim, however, argues that 4Q365 is closer to the proto-rabbinic text in the Tabernacle Sections. A. Kim, "The Textual Alignment of the Tabernacle Sections of 4Q365," 68-69.

Since the context is broken, the exact sequence of thought on the fragment is not clear, but the underlined phrase from line 2 of the fragment, which is unique to 4Q365, seems to be a comment on the strength of the Egyptian army that explains the Israelites' fear earlier in the verse. Exod 14:7 mentions that Pharaoh sent out six hundred chariots after the Israelites; that number is repeated here in the exegetical comment. The number of horses (either two thousand or some other multiple of a thousand; since the context is broken we cannot be sure) is not mentioned in the immediate context of Exodus 14; however, the phrase "two thousand horses" appears in 2 Kgs 18:23 (= Isa 36:8), in the Rabshekah's taunting speech to the Israelites. This reference may have prompted the scribal choice made here in Exodus. As in the example from 4Q364, whether this exegetical comment was added by the scribe of 4Q365 or earlier, we cannot tell.

4Q364 and 4Q365 also contain examples of the type of major harmonistic editing considered characteristic of the group of texts exemplified by the pre-Samaritan text. Once again, however, the major harmonistic changes are not identical to the pre-Samaritan text, indicating that we are witnessing a scribal tradition of harmonizing exegesis, not the phenomenon of one manuscript copying another (although this of course did happen).

The first example of major harmonizing that I want to present from 4Q364 also happens to occur in the Samaritan Pentateuch. It is found in Genesis 30–31, part of the Jacob cycle, in which Jacob tells his wives of the dream he has had prompting him to return to the land of Canaan. In the textual tradition witnessed by the Masoretic Text and the Septuagint, Jacob merely reports to his wives that he has had this dream:

> "At the mating time of the flocks, I raised my eyes and I saw in a dream — the he-goats mating with the flock were striped, speckled, and mottled. And an angel of God said to me in the dream, 'Jacob!' and I said, 'Here I am.' And he said, 'Raise your eyes and see all the he-goats mating with the flocks are striped, speckled, and mottled, because I have seen all that Laban has done to you. I am the god of Bethel, where you anointed a pillar, where you vowed a vow to me. Now, arise, go forth from this land and return to the land of your birth.'" (Gen 31:10-13)

However, we never actually see Jacob having the dream. This leaves an interpretive gap in the text; does Jacob really have the dream he reports, or is he making it up as a convenient excuse to return to Canaan? Since the latter suggestion may cast doubt on the patriarch's rectitude, the harmonistic scribal tradition filled the gap by supplying the dream earlier, in what is now ch. 30. This is how the harmonization appears in 4Q364, frgs. 4b-e, col. ii, lines 18-26:

> (Gen 30:36) [and he (Laban) set a] th[ree-days' journey between himself and Jacob, and Jacob was pasturing[the remainder of] Laban's flock. *vacat* And [the messenger of God] spok[e to Jacob in a dream, and he said, "Jacob!" and he said,] "H[ere I am!" And he said, "Raise]your[eyes, and see all the he-goats mating with the flock are striped, spe]ckled[and mottled, because I have seen all that Laban has done to you. I am the god of Bethel, w]here[you anointed a pillar and where you vowed a vow to me. And now, rise, go forth] f[rom this land and return to the land of your] f[ather, and I will do good with you" . . .]

The careful reader will note that this text is extensively reconstructed in 4Q364. We are able to do this because the same harmonization occurs in the Samaritan Pentateuch, where we have the complete text. The exegetical tradition has taken Jacob's report of his dream to Leah and Rachel in Gen 31:11-13 and repeated it almost verbatim here. This is an anticipatory harmonization; it reassures the reader that Jacob actually had the dream he reports. The fact that it occurs in both 4Q364 and the Samaritan Pentateuch points to a common exegetical tradition.

4Q364 also contains examples of major harmonizations that it does not share with the Samaritan Pentateuch. Since 4Q364 is a fragmentary text, we cannot be entirely certain of the nature and purpose of these harmonizations, but it is fairly clear that harmonizing activity is occurring in the text. We also, of course, are not certain whether the harmonizations were introduced by the scribe of 4Q364 or earlier.

The first example is found on frg. 14, which contains the text of Exod 24:12-14, recounting God's command to Moses to come up to Mount Sinai to receive the tablets of the law. Prior to the Exodus text, however, frg. 14 contains two lines of extremely broken material, unique to 4Q364, ending with the phrase "on the slopes of the mountain" (בתחתית ההר). This same phrase occurs in Exod 19:17, part of the Sinai theophany. In 19:20, God also summons Moses up the mountain. What seems to be happening in 4Q364 is the use of (at least) phrases from the earlier theophany narrated in Exodus 19 before the parallel text in Exodus 24. Since 4Q364 is so fragmentary, and we do not have any other fragments containing Exodus 19, it is also possible that 4Q364 skipped from Exod 19:17 to Exod 24:12, leaving out the intervening chapters. However, the letter remains of frg. 14 do not fit the latter explanation well; there seem to be words on frg. 14 which do not occur in Exod 19:17. Therefore, the suggestion that an otherwise unknown harmonization has occurred seems more likely.

The second example of a harmonization that 4Q364 does not share with the Samaritan Pentateuch occurs in frgs. 23a-b, col. i. This harmonization occurs before the text of Deut 2:8-14. In this passage of Deuteronomy Moses is retelling the story of the Israelites' journey through Transjordan and their avoidance of Edom and Moab. Right before Deut 2:8, 4Q364 inserts a passage from the parallel text in Num 20:14-18:

Num 20:17-18 (MT)	4Q364 (extant)	Deut 2:4-8
		Command the people, saying, "you are crossing the territory of your brethren, the Edomites, who dwell in Seir. They will fear you, but be careful, do not provoke them. For I will not give to you from their land, not so much as a foot can tread. For I have given to Esau Mt. Seir as an inheritance. You shall buy food from them with money, and you shall eat; and likewise water you will purchase from them with money, and you will drink. For the LORD *your God has blessed you in all your doings. He has watched over your wanderings in this great desert these forty years; the* LORD *your God has been with you, you have lacked nothing.*
From Kadesh, Moses sent messengers to the king of Edom: "Thus says your brother Israel: You know all the hardships that have befallen us; that our ancestors went down to Egypt, that we dwelt in Egypt a long time, and that the Egyptians dealt harshly with us and our ancestors.		

Num 20:17-18 (MT)	4Q364 (extant)	Deut 2:4-8
We cried to the LORD and he heard our plea, and he sent a messenger who freed us from Egypt. Now we are in Kadesh, the town on the border of your territory. Let us cross your country. We will not cross in the field or in the vineyard, and we will not drink water from the well; we will go on the King's Road; we will not swerve to the right or left until we reach your border." But Edom said to him, "You shall not cross over me lest with the sword I come out to meet you."	. . . c]ross in the field or in the vineya[rd, and we will n]ot[drink water from the well; we will go on the King's Road;] we will n[ot] swerve to the right or left [until we reach your border." But *he* said,] "You shall not cro[ss over] me lest [with the sword I come out to meet you" . . . *Then we moved away from our brethren, the the children of Esau . . .*	*Then we moved away from our brethren, the children of Esau . . .*

Although 4Q364 is fragmentary, we can see the harmonization that has occurred. Moses' negotiation with the king of Edom, reported in Numbers 20, has been inserted in 4Q364 in the parallel report of the journey in Deuteronomy. What is particularly interesting about this harmonization is that it imports material from Numbers into Deuteronomy. In the tradition exemplified in the pre-Samaritan texts, the normal direction of harmonization is from Deuteronomy into Numbers; in fact, the Samaritan Pentateuch reverses the harmonization of 4Q364 by inserting Deut 2:2-6 after Num 20:13.[6] This example, which shows what is essentially the same harmonization taking place in two ways, demonstrates that we are dealing in these manuscripts with a general tradition of scribal exegesis that could arrive at different results.

4Q365 does not share any large harmonizations with the Samaritan Pentateuch, but it does contain a harmonization similar to one in 4QNum[b], another member of the group of harmonizing, or pre-Samaritan, texts. This harmonization occurs on frg. 36, where Num 27:11 is followed immediately (without even a paragraph break) by Num 36:1-2, the two pericopes in Numbers concerning the inheritance of the daughters of Zelophehad. Since 4Q365 is fragmentary, it is impossible to tell if the passage from ch. 36 has been

---

6. Num 20:13 is not preserved in 4Q364, so we cannot tell whether or not it contained the Samaritan Pentateuch's harmonization. This harmonization is also preserved in 4QNum[b]; Jastram, "4QNum[b]," 225.

transferred to the middle of ch. 27 or whether 27:1-11 has been transferred to the beginning of ch. 36. The preserved text follows:

> (27:11) If [his father] had no[brothers, then you shall give his inheritance to his nearest relative in his clan,] and he shall inherit i[t. This will be the law of procedure for the children of Israel, according as the LORD commanded] Moses. (36:1-2) And[the heads of families belonging to the clans of Gilead son of Machir, son of Manasseh, from the clans] of Joseph drew near before[Moses and before the leaders, the heads of the families belonging to the children of] Israel, and they said, ["The LORD commanded my lord to give the land in inheritance] by lot to[the children of Israel. . . ."

In 4QNum[b], it appears as if part of Numbers 27 has been inserted into Numbers 36, in a slightly different way than in 4Q365.[7] This is another example, from two different manuscripts related to the pre-Samaritan group, of a particular exegetical tradition that manifests itself in different ways in different manuscripts.

Another example of a harmonizing change in 4Q365 is found on frg. 28. This fragment contains the text of Num 4:47-49 (the end of ch. 4), followed by a blank line, then continuing with Num 7:1. The blank line may be a signal to the reader that an exegetical change has occurred, but we cannot be certain. The reason for the joining together of these two passages is that both concern the service of the tabernacle; ch. 4 ends with the census of the Levites to determine who was eligible to serve in the tabernacle; ch. 7 begins with the completion of the tabernacle. The intervening material in chs. 5 and 6 is a miscellaneous collection of laws not relating to the service of the tabernacle; therefore it makes exegetical sense to join the end of ch. 4 with the beginning of ch. 7. Whether 4Q365 completely omitted chs. 5 and 6 or moved their contents to other places in the manuscript we do not know; no fragments of those chapters remain. We also cannot determine if this exegetical change originated with the scribe of 4Q365 or earlier in the tradition.

The Addition of "New" Material into the Text

Thus far we have been discussing the characteristics of 4Q364 and 4Q365 that mark them as part of the group of texts identified as pre-Samaritan, or

---

7. See Jastram, "4QNum[b]," 263-64, who reconstructs the order of the verses as follows: 36:1-2; 27:2-11; 36:3-4; 36:1-2; 36:5-13.

harmonistic. However, 4Q364 and 4Q365, as part of the group of texts called Reworked Pentateuch, move yet a step further along the spectrum. They do this by adding new material into their received text, thereby "hyper-expanding" the text of the Pentateuch. This step along the spectrum is part of the tradition of scribal exegesis we have been discussing, and it does distance these texts still further from the (shorter) texts of the proto-rabbinic group, which do not belong within the same tradition of scribal exegesis.

There are three major examples of this step toward "hyperexpansion" in 4Q364 and 4Q365. The first, in 4Q364, occurs in frg. 3, col. ii. The last two lines of this fragment contain Gen 28:6, which reads "And Esau saw that [Isaac had blessed Jacob and sent him] to Pa[ddan] Aram, to take for himself from[there a wife. . . ." Preceding this verse come six lines of text not known (in its entirety) from other sources. The lines are as follows:

1. him you shall see [
2. you shall see in peace [
3. your death, and to [your] eyes[
4. the two of you. And he called[
5. to her all the wo[rds
6. after Jacob her son[

The lines appear to contain a dialogue between Isaac and Rebekah, in which Rebekah grieves over Jacob's departure and Isaac attempts to comfort her. This additional material is paralleled in a variety of sources available in the Second Temple period. The first is the text of Genesis itself; the phrase "the two of you" echoes the identical phrase in Gen 27:45, in which Rebekah, while sending Jacob away, says to him, "Why should I lose even *the two of you* in one day?"[8] If this had been the only line extant, we would probably surmise that a simple harmonization had occurred. However, the remainder of the lines does not contain echoes of pentateuchal passages, but rather other texts from the period. Jubilees 27, which narrates the same scene as Genesis 28, contains the lines "The spirit of Rebecca was grieved *after Jacob her son*" (Jub 27:14) and "we *see him in peace*" (Jub 27:17). The texts are not exact copies of one another, but certainly point to the same interpretive tradition, manifest in slightly different ways in the two works. As I shall argue in the chapter on Jubilees, the Reworked Pentateuch texts and Jubilees stem from the same scribal tradition.

---

8. Hence, in the *editio princeps* Tov and I filled out line 3 of the fragment with למה אשכל גם from Gen 27:45.

Further, the text in 4Q364 is similar to the scene in the book of Tobit in which Tobit and his wife Anna bid farewell to their son Tobias. Anna weeps over Tobias's departure, but Tobit comforts her, promising her *"your eyes will see him* on the day when he returns to you *in peace"* (Tob 5:21). The similarities between the two texts, in vocabulary and scenario, are striking. The book of Tobit was found in five manuscripts at Qumran. A common exegetical tradition seems to be at work among these three texts.

4Q365 contains two large additions, at different points in the text and of different types. One of these additions is narrative in nature, the other legal.[9] The first occurs in frgs. 6a-c, col. ii, in the text of Exodus 15. Frg. 6b (part of col. i) of 4Q365 contains Exod 15:16-20 in its extant text. Since we do not have the bottom of the fragment, it is likely that the text continued through v. 21. Verse 22 begins on line 8 of frg. 6a, col. ii. Between v. 21, which begins at the end of col. i, and v. 22, which commences on line 8 of col. ii, intervene at least seven lines of text not found in any other witness to the text of Exodus. The lines read as follows:

1. you despised [
2. for the majesty of[
3. You are great, O deliverer [
4. the hope of the enemy has perished, and he has cea[sed/is forgotten. . . .
5. they perished in the mighty waters, the enemy[
6. Extol the one who raises up, [a ra]nsom you gave[
7. [do]ing gloriously[

Given the position of these lines on col. ii, it is clear that they are the fragmentary remains of a Song of Miriam, added into the text of Exodus 15 after the snippet of song that Miriam sings in 15:21, a mere repetition of the first verse of the song that Moses sings in 15:1-18. The addition was prompted by what could be perceived as an interpretive gap in the text: did Miriam only repeat the refrain of Moses' song, or did she sing a longer song? 4Q365 answers the latter question affirmatively, in the ancient tradition of victory songs sung by women.[10]

The additional material draws on the Song of Moses as its primary in-

---

9. Bernstein notes that 4QRP differs from the pre-Samaritan tradition in its willingness to intervene in legal as well as narrative passages. Bernstein, "What Has Happened to the Laws?" This observation strengthens my argument that the Reworked Pentateuch group occupies a position a step further along the spectrum of Rewritten Scriptures texts.

10. Compare Deborah in Judges 5, Hannah in 1 Samuel 2, and Judith in Judith 16; for a discussion of these songs in relation to the Song of Miriam, see Brooke, "Power to the Powerless."

spiration: the phrase "in the mighty waters" is repeated from 15:10, and the root *g-'-h*, here translated as "majesty" (line 2) and "gloriously" (line 7), occurs in 15:1, 7, and 21. In addition to the Song of Moses, the scribe(s) drew on other texts to construct Miriam's Song: the phrase "you are great" occurs in Jer 10:6 and Ps 86:10; "the hope of the enemy has perished" bears a resemblance to Prov 10:28, "and the hope of the wicked will perish"; and "[do]ing gloriously" resembles Isa 12:5: "he has done gloriously." Finally, there may be connections at the level of motif to other women's victory songs like Judith 16 and the later Magnificat of Mary in Luke 1. These motifs are the greatness of God and the elevation of the weak through God's action.[11]

Thus, the Song of Miriam is clearly the product of scribal exegesis; it demonstrates the skilful use of other texts to create something new, something that fills an interpretive gap in the received text. This Song does not reappear in other parts of the Jewish tradition; Josephus and the rabbis have no knowledge of it, and it disappeared until its rediscovery in Cave 4.

The second major addition preserved in 4Q365 is found on frg. 23. This fragment begins with Lev 23:42–24:2. Leviticus 23 contains a festival calendar, which ends in v. 44 with "Thus Moses declared the festivals of the LORD to the children of Israel." That is, according to the Torah, the festivals enumerated in ch. 23 are the only festivals that God commanded to Moses on Mount Sinai. However, in the course of time in the Second Temple period the Jewish festival calendar had expanded, raising the question of whether or not these new festivals were in fact ordained by God. The festivals of Purim and Hanukkah began to be celebrated in the late Second Temple period by some but not all groups of Jews. For example, there is no evidence that the Essene community who lived at Qumran celebrated either festival. One of the reasons for this is that neither festival originated with Moses; Purim is associated with the book of Esther, while Hanukkah comes about during the period of the Maccabees in the second century B.C.E. However, the Qumran group did celebrate other festivals that are not found in the received text of Leviticus, such as the harvest festivals of New Wine and New Oil. How were these evidently non-Mosaic festivals justified?

One answer may be found in frg. 23 of 4Q365, which illustrates an interpretive tradition in which the newer festivals were "discovered" by exegesis from the existing festivals and thus given the Mosaic imprimatur. Fragment 23 gives the continuous text of Leviticus from 23:42–24:1, but suddenly, after beginning 24:2, it switches without warning and without mark to material that is otherwise unknown to Leviticus. In other words, the scribe(s) is using the received text of Leviticus as a vehicle for exegesis and is hyperexpanding

11. Brooke, "Power to the Powerless," 64.

it. This is not "new composition," but a handing on of the book of Leviticus as interpreted within a particular legal tradition, a priestly-levitical legal tradition we will find in other Qumran scrolls (see below). The expansion fills in an interpretive gap in the mind of the reader, if not the text: if these festivals we celebrate are not mentioned in the Law of Moses, why do we celebrate them? The expansion answers the question by finding the justification for the new festivals within the festival calendar in Leviticus 23. The scribe(s) adds regulations concerning the wood offering for the temple, which evidently follows the festival of New Oil. The latter is a harvest festival, a natural continuation of the "sheaf of first fruits," which was associated with the barley harvest, and the harvest festival of grain already enumerated in Lev 23:10-14, 15-21. The wood offering is a necessity for the sacrifices in the temple and is mentioned in the book of Nehemiah (10:35; 13:31), where, however, the offering is collected differently. 4Q365's text reads as follows, beginning with line 4:

4. and the LORD spoke to Moses, saying, "Command the children of Israel, saying, when you come to the land which

5. I am giving to you for an inheritance, and you dwell upon it securely, you will gather wood for the burnt offering and for all the wor[k] of

6. [the h]ouse which you will build for me in the land, to arrange them upon the altar of the burnt offering [and] the calv[e]s

7. .] . . for Passover sacrifices and for whole burnt-offerings and for thank offerings and for free-will offerings and for burnt-offerings, daily[

8. . . .] . . . and for the d[o]ors and for all the work of the house, [they] will brin[g . . .

9. . . . fe]stival of New Oil, they will bring the wood two[. . .

10. . . .] those who bring on the fir[s]t day, Levi [. . .

11. . . . Reu]ben and Simeon[and on the] four[th] day [. . .

The festival of New Oil is known from other Qumran documents, including 4QCalendrical Document E and 4QMMT A. A wood offering for the temple in various forms found a wider currency in Second Temple Judaism, being mentioned in Josephus (*War* 2.425) and rabbinic literature (*Meg. Ta'an.* 4.5). Jubilees 21 discusses the types of wood appropriate for the temple sacrifices.

However, these lines of text from 4Q365 find their closest parallel in the Temple Scroll. The Temple Scroll also legislates for the festival of New Oil (cols. 11, 21-22, and 43); according to the Temple Scroll, the date of the festival is the 22nd day of the sixth month, right before the six-day Wood Festival. That date (or at least the proximity of the two festivals) seems to agree with 4Q365, frg. 23, which mentions the festival of New Oil in line 9, then goes on immediately to discuss the Wood Festival, also evidently a six-day festival (since lines 10 and 11 mention the first and fourth days).

Even more important are the parallels between these lines and cols. 23 and 24 of the Temple Scroll, which treat the Wood Festival. According to the Temple Scroll, the Wood Festival lasts for six days, from the 23rd to the 29th of the sixth month. This differs from the traditions of Nehemiah, Josephus, and the rabbis, but agrees with frg. 23, which envisions the tribes bringing the offering on consecutive days (lines 9-11). The most striking parallel between 4Q365 and the Temple Scroll is in fact in the order in which the tribes bring the offering. The Temple Scroll gives the following order: Levi and Judah on the first day, Benjamin and Joseph on the second, Reuben and Simeon on the third, Issachar and Zebulun on the fourth, Gad and Asher on the fifth, and Dan and Naphtali on the sixth day. In its complete form this tribal order is unique; it is not found elsewhere in extant Jewish literature. However, it does seem to be the same order found in fragmentary form on frg. 23: Levi on the first day and Reuben and Simeon on the third. This parallel between the Temple Scroll and 4Q365 led some scholars, beginning with Yigael Yadin, to include frg. 23 as part of a copy of the Temple Scroll.[12] However, as I have shown in a previous publication, although the contents of frg. 23 are a close parallel to the text of cols. 23-24 of the Temple Scroll, a detailed examination demonstrates that they are not copies of the same text.[13] Rather, it is possible that 4Q365, frg. 23 contains material that served as a source for the author/redactor of the Temple Scroll.[14] At the very least, frg. 23's overlap with the Temple Scroll demonstrates that the two documents are part of the same exegetical tradition. Further, that exegetical tradition carried authority with at least one group of Jews in the late Second Temple period, since other documents from Qumran (4QCalendrical Document E, 4QMMT) mention the festival of New Oil. This, as we shall see, is the strongest evidence for the scriptural authority of (this manuscript of) Reworked Pentateuch.

We have been discussing the major instances of hyperexpansion in 4Q364 and 4Q365. There is, however, evidence of a more fragmentary nature that this type of scribal activity was widespread throughout the two manuscripts. For example, 4Q365, frg. 26a-b contains the end of the book of Leviticus and the beginning of the book of Numbers on the same fragment. This is part of the evidence for the claim that these manuscripts were copies of the

---

12. Yadin, *Megillat ha-Miqdash*, 3:pl. 40*, 1.

13. Crawford, "Three Fragments from Qumran Cave 4," 261-65.

14. Wise, *A Critical Study of the Temple Scroll*, 49-50; Crawford, *The Temple Scroll and Related Texts*, 55.

entire Pentateuch. Line 1 contains the phrase "children of Israel," which is part of Lev 27:34, the last verse of Leviticus. Line 3 is a blank line; line 4 begins with Num 1:1. Therefore it is reasonable to conclude that this fragment represents the end of Leviticus and the beginning of Numbers. However, line 2 contains the remains of words that do not occur in the received text of Leviticus. Therefore, it is likely that frg. 26 contained an exegetical addition at the end of the book of Leviticus, even though we are unable to reconstruct it.

Other Examples of the Reworked Pentateuch Group: 4Q158

4Q364 and 4Q365 are the main exemplars of the group Reworked Pentateuch because they are the most extensively preserved. Other, smaller manuscripts fall into this category as well.

4Q158 consists of 15 fragments which contain parts of Genesis and Exodus and two short passages from Deuteronomy. The date of the manuscript is the middle of the first century B.C.E. Although 4Q158 overlaps with other manuscripts in the Reworked Pentateuch group in several places, none of these overlaps indicate that 4Q158 is a direct copy of any of the others.[15] Therefore, I prefer to think of 4Q158 as another member of the group Reworked Pentateuch rather than to speak of copies.[16] The evidence for placing 4Q158 in this group is solid.

4Q158 demonstrates many of the same features as 4Q364 and 4Q365. Some of the manuscript fragments of 4Q158 contain texts that do not differ substantially from the received text of Exodus, e.g., frgs. 5 (Exod 19:17-23) and 9 (Exod 21:15-25). Some fragments demonstrate that 4Q158 had a text that was part of the pre-Samaritan group, e.g., frg. 6, which interpolates into the account of the Mount Sinai theophany in Exodus 20 elements from the parallel account in Deut 5:28-31, as well as Deut 18:18-22. This text is the same as the Samaritan Pentateuch's version of Exod 20:19-22; in other words, 4Q158 shares the same scribal tradition as the pre-Samaritan group.

However, 4Q158 also moves beyond the pre-Samaritan group with the same kind of exegetical activity we have already observed in 4Q364 and 4Q365. 4Q158 interprets the received text according to its own exegetical principles. For example, Gen 32:25-32 (Jacob wrestling with the angel) and Exod 4:27-28 (Moses' meeting with Aaron when he returns from Midian) appear to be juxtaposed on frgs. 1-2. Here is the text of the fragments, beginning with Gen 32:30 in line 6:

15. Tov and White, "Reworked Pentateuch," 190-91.
16. Also Brooke, "4Q158: Reworked Pentateuch^a or Reworked Pentateuch A?".

6. . . . J[a]cob then asked him, "Please [te]ll me [your name."
7. [And he bles]sed him there. And he said to him, "May the Lo[RD] make you fruitful [and multiply] you[. . .
8. [kn]owledge and understanding, and may he deliver you from all violence and[. . .
9. until this day and for everlast[ing] generations[. . ."
10. And he walked on his way when he blessed him there. (32:31) And he ca[lled . . .
11. (32) to him the sun as he passed Penue[l . . .
12. on that day, and he said to him, "You shall not e[at . . .
13. (33) on the hip sockets to th[is day . . .
14. (Exod 4:27) to Aaron, saying, "Go to mee[t . . .
15. (28) the words of the LORD which he had s[ent] him, and all [the signs . . .
16. the LORD to me, saying, "When you bring forth the[. . .
17. to go as slaves, and behold, they are thirt[y . . .
18. the LORD God[. . .
19. draw off[

The reason for this juxtaposition, seen in lines 13 and 14, is not entirely clear; unlike the other harmonizations we have studied, the juxtaposition of Genesis 32 and Exodus 4 does not seem to fill an interpretive gap in the text, nor do the texts at first glance seem to relate to the same topic. Further, these fragments in 4Q158 are not merely harmonistic, but also hyperexpansive. This is most clearly demonstrated in lines 7-10, which come at the end of Gen 32:30. These lines add new text containing the content of the angel's blessing of Jacob, not found in any other witness. The hyperexpansion fills an interpretive gap in the text, namely the contents of the angelic blessing. Like the Song of Miriam in 4Q365, this exegetical expansion borrows language from blessings found elsewhere in what became the biblical text, e.g. Gen 1:28; 17:6; 28:3, and the expansion functions in the same way.

Interestingly, it is possible that 4Q364 contained this same expansion. Frg. 5b, col. ii of 4Q364 contains the text of Gen 32:26-30. Line 13 contains the last letter of the word "there" (שם); it then continues with "and he sai[d" (ויואמ[ר]). This is the same word that begins the expansion in line 7 of 4Q158. Gen 32:31, on the other hand, begins with "and he called" (ויקרא), found in 4Q158 on line 10. Since 4Q158 and 4Q364 both contain the word "and he said" (ויואמר) at a point in the text where 4Q158 begins an expansion, it is entirely possible that 4Q364 contained the same expansion. If it did, this would be strong proof of a filial relationship between 4Q158 and 4Q364, more evidence that we are dealing with one single line of exegetical tradition. Unfortunately, 4Q364 breaks off at this point, so we cannot be certain.

The text following the expansion in lines 7-10 of 4Q158 gives further evidence of scribal exegesis. Lines 11-12 contain the text of Gen 32:31-32. Line 13 is similar in content to Gen 32:33, but the first extant phrase, "on that day" (ביום ההואה), does not occur in the other witnesses to Genesis. The next section, beginning with "and he said," couches the prohibition of the consumption of the thigh sinew as a direct command rather than the indirect explanation found in the received text. The reason for these variations from the received text is not immediately apparent, except to make the alimentary prohibition direct and unmistakable. We also do not know whether or not these lines originated with the scribe of 4Q158.

Finally, although line 14 seems to indicate that 4Q158 has jumped to Exod 4:27 ("and the LORD said to Aaron . . ."), the following lines contain another reworked text. Lines 16-19 do not contain material found in the received text of Exodus, but rather contain a text which draws elements from Exodus 3. To illustrate, in line 16 Moses seems to be reporting to Aaron what God said to him in Exod 3:12, repeating the phrase "when you bring forth the people" (בהוציאכה אתן העם). Line 17 contains the phrase "to go as slaves," a reference to the Exodus, and contains the word "thirty" or "three," which may refer either to the length of the Israelites' sojourn in Egypt[17] or to the three days' journey into the wilderness in Exod 3:18.[18] Finally, line 19 contains the word "draw off," which occurs in the imperative in Exod 3:5, where God commands Moses to remove his sandals. All this information points to a reworked text, which again fills in an interpretive gap in the received text: when Exod 4:28 says that "Moses told Aaron all the words of the LORD . . . ," what did Moses say? 4Q158 answers the question by reconstructing Moses' encounter with God prior to meeting Aaron. This kind of harmonistic exegesis is in keeping with the pre-Samaritan tradition, and worked out to an even greater extent in the Reworked Pentateuch texts.

The major difficulty that presents itself with the study of these fragments is understanding the connection between the Genesis and Exodus passages. First, the fragment begins with a reworked text, so we cannot be certain of its context. Lines 1-3 are very fragmentary. None of the preserved words coincide with either Gen 32:22-24, the verses that preceded Gen 32:25 in the received text, or Exod 4:24-26, the passage that precedes Exod 4:27. We therefore cannot presume that our fragment contained a running text of Genesis with

17. Strugnell, "Notes en marge," 169-70.
18. Segal, "Biblical Exegesis in 4Q158," 59.

an interpolation from Exodus or a running text of Exodus with an interpolation from Genesis. The words "you have fought" (שרית) on line 2 do occur in Gen 32:29 (the same words are not preserved in 4Q158, line 6). It is possible that lines 1-2 contain an exegetical expansion based on the following material, but it is impossible to be certain. Second, we are not certain of the context of the end of the fragment either. If the reworked text at the end of the fragment is meant to occur after Genesis 32, with Genesis 33 continuing afterward, then Moses and Aaron are introduced out of chronological sequence and the connection between the received texts and the expansion is ambiguous.

There are two possibilities for understanding the sequence of passages. One is that the promise given to Jacob by the angel in the exegetical expansion in lines 7-10, that God would deliver his descendants from violence, is seen as fulfilled in the Exodus from Egypt, so that God's statement to Moses in Exodus 3 about the pending deliverance is paraphrased here out of sequence to indicate the fulfillment of the promise. The chronological difficulty mentioned above, however, remains. The second possibility for understanding the sequence is that the passage from Genesis has been inserted into Exodus (rather than vice versa), so that the Genesis pericope would follow the story of Moses' and Zipporah's encounter with (the angel of) God in Exod 4:24-26, a story that also involves the possibility of harm to the protagonist. This possibility of harm would be the exegetical "hook" that led the scribe to insert the Genesis story at this point in the Exodus narrative.[19] The weakness of this second possibility is that there is no actual quotation or reworking of Exod 4:24-26 (as stated above), leaving the connection to be guessed at. Neither solution is entirely satisfactory; therefore, it must be said that the reason for the particular sequence of passages in frgs. 1-2 remains elusive.

These two small fragments of 4Q158 contain all the characteristics of the group we call the Reworked Pentateuch texts. In fact, 4Q158 shows evidence of more extensive scribal exegesis than either 4Q364 or 4Q365, indicating that we could refine the spectrum of texts endlessly. For convenience, however, it is better to consider these texts as members of one group.[20]

We have examined three examples from the category Reworked Pentateuch texts. It is clear from this examination that these manuscripts belong in the scribal tradition that created the pre-Samaritan group of Pentateuch texts, with their primary trait of harmonization. However, these texts move beyond the pre-Samaritan group in their practice of exegesis by creating new

19. Tov, "Biblical Texts as Reworked in Some Qumran Manuscripts," 131-32; Segal, "Biblical Exegesis in 4Q158," 48.

20. Brooke, "4Q158: Reworked Pentateuch^a or Reworked Pentateuch A?", 219.

material, additions which not only fill interpretive gaps in the received text, but also expand the text for theological reasons (i.e. 4Q365, frg. 23). Thus I have called these texts "hyperexpansive."

The Question of Authority

We raised the question of the status and authority of these texts at the beginning of the chapter. Were these manuscripts considered as Scripture by any group of Jews, in particular the group at Qumran, at any point in time? Unfortunately we cannot be completely sure of the answer. If these texts (especially 4Q364 and 4Q365, which were manuscripts of the entire Pentateuch when whole) were considered simply as part of an ongoing tradition of exegesis of the Pentateuch, then these manuscripts were probably accepted as exemplars of the Five Books of Moses, carrying the full weight and authority of the Torah. This is the position of Eugene Ulrich, Michael Segal, Armin Lange, and now also Emanuel Tov.[21] Arguments in favor of this position are, first, the fact that these manuscripts evidently present themselves in the same way as those manuscripts we now categorize as "biblical," that is, as regular Torah manuscripts. For example, the Tetragrammaton (the consonants of the Divine Name YHWH) is written in square script,[22] and there is no distinction made between new exegetical text and the received text, indicating that the entire text was meant to be considered part of the Torah. So we can say with almost complete certainty that 4Q364 and 4Q365 were meant by the scribes who prepared them to be read as regular pentateuchal texts. This is one of the criteria for scriptural status discussed in the Introduction above.[23] Second, the category has yielded several examples from the Qumran caves, indicating that this type of text was popular at least in the Qumran community. The number of copies is considered a weak indicator of scriptural status. Finally, there are suggestions that both 4Q364 and 4Q365 share a tradition of exegesis found in Jubilees and the Temple Scroll. The question is raised, could 4Q364 have been a source for Jubilees, and/or 4Q365 for the

---

21. Ulrich, "The Qumran Scrolls and the Biblical Text"; Segal, "4QReworked Pentateuch or 4QPentateuch?"; Lange, "The Status of the Biblical Texts," 27; Tov, "Reflections on the Many Forms of Hebrew Scripture in Light of the LXX and 4Q Reworked Pentateuch." I would like to thank Professor Tov for sharing this paper with me prior to its publication.

22. 4Q364 has the unique practice of inserting a scribal mark resembling a colon (:) before each occurrence of the Tetragrammaton. This may have been a device to warn the reader not to pronounce the Divine Name.

23. The same may be true for the other texts included in this category, although there is no evidence for this from their fragments.

Temple Scroll? If it could be shown without doubt that Jubilees used 4Q364, frg. 3, col. ii (the Isaac/Rebekah passage) as a source, or that the Temple Scroll used 4Q365, frg. 23 (the New Oil/Wood Festival passage) as a source, then the argument for the authoritative status of these manuscripts would be greatly strengthened, since this would indicate community acceptance of a Reworked Pentateuch manuscript as authoritative. The evidence is unfortunately not definitive that either 4Q364 was used as a source by Jubilees or 4Q365 by the Temple Scroll; the passages in question are not exact copies of one another, and there are several important differences. The most that can be said with certainty is that all these manuscripts shared a common tradition of exegesis, and that this tradition of exegesis was authoritative in and of itself, at least for those groups that embraced it. However, the evidence for the authoritative status of at least some of the manuscripts within the Reworked Pentateuch group in the community of Jews at Qumran is not certain, and becomes slimmer as the manuscripts become more fragmentary.[24] What is more, texts from the Reworked Pentateuch group do not continue to be copied; they do not survive the Great Jewish Revolt, and no single text from the group is canonized by any subsequent community. At the same time, the *pesher* genre, characterized by commentary separate from the received text, first appears in this same period, the first century B.C.E.[25] We may have in the Reworked Pentateuch group the end of a very long tradition of innerscriptural scribal exegesis, soon to be replaced by another tradition of separating the authoritative text from its commentary, a tradition that survives to our own day.

The Reworked Pentateuch group contains the latest chronological examples of this tradition of scribal exegesis, in which the scribe's work did not result in a new composition. In the next examples along our spectrum of Rewritten Scripture works, Jubilees and the Temple Scroll, the scribal redaction results in new compositions, clearly differentiated from the Pentateuch.

We will probably never be certain of the status of these Reworked Pentateuch texts as Torah in the late Second Temple period.[26] However, we can firmly say that their tradition of interpretation was accepted as authoritative by one stream of Judaism in the Second Temple period. This tradition of priestly-levitical scribal exegesis begins in the pre-Samaritan texts, continues in the Reworked Pentateuch group, and, as we shall see, moves on into Jubilees, the Temple Scroll, and the Genesis Apocryphon.

---

24. Bernstein, "What Has Happened to the Laws," considers it "very unlikely" that at least some of the manuscripts should be considered an edition of the Pentateuch."
25. Brooke, "The Rewritten Law, Prophets and Psalms," 38.
26. This is also the position of Falk, *The Parabiblical Texts*, 119.

BIBLIOGRAPHY

Allegro, John M. "Biblical Paraphrase: Genesis, Exodus." In *Qumrân Cave 4.I (4Q158-4Q186)*, 1-6. DJD 5. Oxford: Clarendon, 1968.

Bernstein, Moshe. "What Happened to the Laws? The Treeatment of the Legal Material in 4QReworked Pentateuch," *DSD* (forthcoming). I would like to thank Professor Bernstein for sharing his manuscript with me prior to publication.

Brooke, George J. "4Q158: Reworked Pentateuch[a] or Reworked Pentateuch A?" *DSD* 8 (2001) 219-41.

————. "Power To the Powerless: A Long-Lost Song of Miriam." *BAR* 20/3 (1994) 62-65.

————. "The Rewritten Law, Prophets and Psalms: Issues for Understanding the Text of the Bible." In *The Bible as Book: The Hebrew Bible and the Judaean Desert Discoveries*, ed. Edward D. Herbert and Emanuel Tov, 31-40. London: British Library and New Castle, DE: Oak Knoll, 2002.

Crawford, Sidnie White. *The Temple Scroll and Related Texts*. Companion to the Qumran Scrolls 2. Sheffield: Sheffield Academic, 2000.

————. "Three Fragments from Qumran Cave 4 and Their Relationship to the Temple Scroll." *JQR* 85 (1994) 259-73.

Falk, Daniel K. *The Parabiblical Texts: Strategies for Extending the Scriptures Among the Dead Sea Scrolls*. LSTS 63. London: T. & T. Clark, 2007. This work appeared after my manuscript had reached the press, so I was unable to incorporate fully its conclusions in my work.

Jastram, Nathan. "4QNum[b]." In *Qumran Cave 4.VII: Genesis to Numbers*, ed. Eugene Ulrich, Frank Moore Cross, *et al.*, 205-68. DJD 12. Oxford: Clarendon, 1994.

Kim, Angela. "The Textual Alignment of the Tabernacle Sections of 4Q365." *Textus* 21 (2002) 45-69.

Lange, Armin. "The Status of the Biblical Texts in the Qumran Corpus and the Canonical Process." In *The Bible as Book: The Hebrew Bible and the Judaean Desert Discoveries*, ed. Edward D. Herbert and Emanuel Tov, 21-30. London: British Library and New Castle, DE: Oak Knoll, 2002.

Segal, Michael H. "Biblical Exegesis in 4Q158: Techniques and Genre." *Textus* 19 (1998) 45-62.

————. "4QReworked Pentateuch or 4QPentateuch?" In *The Dead Sea Scrolls Fifty Years After Their Discovery*, ed. Lawrence H. Schiffman, Emanuel Tov, and James C. VanderKam, 391-99. Jerusalem: Israel Exploration Society, 2000.

Strugnell, John. "Notes en marge du Volume V des 'Discoveries in the Judaean Desert of Jordan.'" *RevQ* 7 (1969-1970) 163-276.

Tov, Emanuel. "Biblical Texts as Reworked in Some Qumran Manuscripts with Special Attention to 4QRP and 4QParaGen-Exod." In *The Community of the Renewed Covenant,* ed. Eugene C. Ulrich and James C. VanderKam, 111-34. Notre Dame: University of Notre Dame Press, 1994.

————. "Reflections on the Many Forms of Hebrew Scripture in Light of the LXX and 4QReworked Pentateuch." In *From Qumran to Aleppo: A Discussion with Emanuel Tov about the Textual History of Jewish Scriptures in Honor of His 65th Birthday,* ed. J. Zsengeller. Leiden: E. J. Brill, 2008.

————, and Sidnie White (Crawford). "Reworked Pentateuch." In *Qumran Cave 4. VIII: Parabiblical Texts, Part 1,* ed. Harold Attridge, T. Elgvin, *et al.,* 187-352. DJD 13. Oxford: Clarendon, 1994.

Ulrich, Eugene C. "The Qumran Scrolls and the Biblical Text." In *The Dead Sea Scrolls Fifty Years After Their Discovery,* ed. Lawrence H. Schiffman, Emanuel Tov, and James C. VanderKam, 51-59. Jerusalem: Israel Exploration Society, 2000.

Wise, Michael O. *A Critical Study of the Temple Scroll from Qumran Cave 11.* SAOC 49. Chicago: University of Chicago Press, 1990.

Yadin, Yigael. *Megillat ha-Miqdash (The Temple Scroll).* 3 vols. Jerusalem: Israel Exploration Society, 1977; rev. Eng. ed., 1983.

CHAPTER 4

The Book of Jubilees

The book of Jubilees is the only document discussed in this volume that was known prior to the discoveries at Qumran. It was preserved especially in the Abyssinian (Ethiopian) Orthodox Church, in which it is part of their canon. Jubilees survived in its entirety only in Ethiopic translation, although fragments survived in Greek, Syriac, and Latin. It was long suspected, however, that Jubilees was originally written in Hebrew or Aramaic, a suspicion confirmed by the discovery of at least 14 and possibly 15 Hebrew manuscripts of Jubilees at Qumran. These manuscripts were distributed among several caves; this and the number of manuscripts preserved attest to the popularity of Jubilees at Qumran. In addition, three manuscripts from Cave 4 have been labeled "pseudo-Jubilees" because of their similarity to the Ethiopic book of Jubilees. Jubilees was translated from Hebrew into Greek; the Greek title was the "Little Genesis." It was translated from Greek into Latin and Ethiopic and into Syriac, either directly from Hebrew or from Greek.[1]

Scriptural Status

Within the Qumran community Jubilees appears to have had the authority of scriptural status. As we shall see, the book certainly presents itself as given by God and thus authoritative: it claims to have been dictated to Moses by an "angel of the presence" on Mount Sinai (Jub 1:4-6, 27). Therefore it meets one of the criteria for scriptural status set out in the Introduction above. Further,

---

1. VanderKam, *The Book of Jubilees* (2001), 11-17.

at least two other documents found at Qumran, the Damascus Document (CD) and 4QText with a Citation of Jubilees (4Q228), cite Jubilees as an authoritative book. The Damascus Document reveals the title of the book in antiquity: "The Book of the Divisions of the Times according to their Jubilees and their Weeks" (CD 16:3-4). This title also appears in a broken context in 4QApocryphon of Jeremiah[b] (4Q384, frg. 9, line 2). Thus Jubilees fulfills another criterion for scriptural status, citation in another text as an authority. Since Jubilees was composed before the foundation of the Qumran community (see below), it is not a Qumran composition but is part of a constellation of texts found at Qumran that share certain priestly-levitical concerns and traits, including, as we have said before, concern for the temple and its rituals, strict purity regulations, and an embrace of a particular chronology and calendar system. These texts were congenial to the Essene movement in the late Second Temple period, of which the Qumran community was a part. Of these texts, which included the books of Enoch, Aramaic Levi (see below), and probably the Temple Scroll (see Chapter 5), we have the most solid evidence for the scriptural status of Jubilees. This status may have continued in the early Christian Church, since Jubilees is cited many times by the church fathers, e.g., Epiphanius, Justin Martyr, Origen, etc.[2] However, Jubilees was not canonized by either Judaism or Christianity, except in the Abyssinian Orthodox Church.

Genre and Date

Prior to the discoveries at Qumran, Jubilees was classified as part of the Jewish Pseudepigrapha, a rather slippery term. In its widest sense it denotes virtually all Jewish works from the Second Temple period outside of the Hebrew Bible, the Apocrypha, Philo, and Josephus. A more narrow definition of "pseudepigrapha" denotes works written in the name of another, more ancient authority, such as Enoch, Levi, or, in the case of Jubilees, Moses. Jubilees fits this second definition, since it purports to be written by Moses, dictated to him by an angel of the presence on Mount Sinai (Jub 1:1–2:1). Its closest comparison before the Qumran discoveries was with the *Liber Antiquitatum Biblicarum* of Pseudo-Philo, a work of the late first century c.e. preserved in Latin.

Now, however, with our vastly expanded knowledge of the variety of Jewish literature in the late Second Temple period, Jubilees can be contex-

---

2. VanderKam, *The Book of Jubilees* (2001), 148.

tualized and classified with more exactitude. Jubilees belongs to the category Rewritten Scripture, located at the point on our spectrum where the act of scribal intervention into a base text(s) becomes so extensive that a new, distinctive composition is created. That is, Jubilees does not simply expand the Pentateuch using the techniques of innerscriptural exegesis, like 4QReworked Pentateuch, but uses the Pentateuchal books of Genesis and Exodus as a base text to create a new composition. The resulting new composition is still closely tied to Genesis and Exodus, in narrative sequence, characters, and content, but Jubilees is a separate book, meant as a companion to the Pentateuch, given to Moses on Sinai at the same time and bearing the same weight of authority. That it was not meant to replace the Torah as the authoritative Jewish law book is clear from its frequent mention of the "First Law" (e.g., Jub 2:24; 6:22; 30:12; 30:21; 50:6), which refers to the Torah.[3] But Jubilees was meant to stand beside that First Law, and it too claims divine authority. Why the composer and his audience thought this second book was necessary will become clear below.

We can set the date of Jubilees' composition with some certainty. A scholarly consensus has formed that Jubilees was composed in the middle of the second century B.C.E. (between 170-150), although there is still considerable disagreement about a more exact date. The earliest manuscript of Jubilees (4Q216) has a paleographical date between 125 and 100 B.C.E.;[4] since there is no reason to suppose that it is the autograph, the very late second-century B.C.E. date proposed by R. H. Charles and others early in the 20th century is no longer tenable. The book's strong polemic against mixing with Gentiles in any way indicates a time period when Jewish-Gentile interaction was perceived by at least some Jewish groups as a threat to Jewish identity. This situation obtained in the mid-second century B.C.E. during the Hellenistic reform in Jerusalem and the subsequent revolt led by the Maccabees (but prior to the establishment of the Hasmonaean dynasty[5]). Thus Jubilees is a work composed in Palestine before the settlement at Qumran was established, but copied and preserved by the Jewish community living there. Jubilees is a unified composition; it was composed or redacted together by one scribe, although the composer certainly used numerous sources for the traditions he interweaves in his book.[6]

3. Najman, 43-50.
4. VanderKam and Milik, "Jubilees," 2.
5. VanderKam, *The Book of Jubilees* (2001), 21.
6. M. Segal has recently proposed a theory of sources discernible in Jubilees. His book (Segal, *The Book of Jubilees*, 2007) was published after this manuscript had gone to press, so I was unable to incoporate fully his work into my own.

Description of the Contents

The book of Jubilees retells the narrative found in the first quarter of the Pentateuch, beginning with the story of creation in Genesis 1 and concluding with Exodus 14, the story of the Passover and the flight from Egypt. The book ends with Moses on Mount Sinai, ready to receive the revelation of the Law (Exodus 24). In Genesis and Exodus the narrative voice is anonymous; although later tradition assigns the authorship of these books to Moses, there is no direct claim in these chapters that they were written by Moses (or anyone else). In Jubilees, however, the claim to divine authority mediated through Moses is made in its first chapter. Jubilees opens, not with the creation as in Genesis 1, but with God's command to Moses to ascend Mount Sinai to receive the law. The prologue reads, "These are the words regarding the divisions of the times of the law and of the testimony, of the events of the years, of the weeks of their jubilees throughout all the years of eternity as he related (them) to Moses on Mt. Sinai when he went up to receive the stone tablets — the law and the commandments — on the Lord's orders as he had told him that he should come up to the summit of the mountain."[7] The setting is essentially taken from Exod 24:12-18, but the composer also draws on the language of the other Sinai theophanies in Exodus (i.e., Exod 19:16-25; 34:1-8) as well as the theological language of Deuteronomy. For example, Jub 1:1b-4a is clearly using Exod 24:12; 15-18 as its base, although it does not quote it exactly:

Jub 1:1b-4a	Exod 24:12, 15-18
The Lord said to Moses, "Come up to me on the mountain.	The LORD said to Moses, "Come up to me on the mountain, and wait there;
I will give you the two stone tablets of the law and the commandments which I have written so that you may teach them." So Moses went up the mountain of the Lord.	and I will give you the tablets of stone, with the law and the commandment, which I have written for their instruction." Then Moses went up on the mountain,
	and the cloud covered the mountain.
The glory of the Lord took up residence on Mount Sinai, and a cloud covered it for six days. When he summoned Moses into the cloud on the seventh day, he saw the	The glory of the LORD settled on Mount Sinai, and the cloud covered it for six days; on the seventh day he called to Moses out of the cloud. Now the appearance of the

7. All translations (with some modifications) are taken from VanderKam, *The Book of Jubilees* (1989).

Jub 1:1b-4a	Exod 24:12, 15-18
glory of the Lord like	glory of the LORD was like
a fire blazing on the summit of the mountain.	a devouring fire on the top of the mountain in the sight of the people of Israel.
	Moses entered the cloud, and went up on
Moses remained on the mountain	the mountain. Moses was on the mountain
for forty days and forty nights. . . .	for forty days and forty nights.

Following the setting of the stage in the language of Exodus, the language of Deuteronomy appears in God's speech to Moses, e.g. at 1:7-8:

Jub 1:7-8	Deut 31:20-21a
which I promised by oath to Abraham, Isaac and Jacob:	
"To your posterity I will give	"For when I have brought them into
the land which flows with milk and honey.	the land flowing with milk and honey, which I promised on oath to their ancestors,
When they eat and are full,	and they have eaten their fill and grown
they will turn	fat, they will turn
to foreign gods — to ones which	to other gods and serve them, despising me and breaking my covenant.
will not save them from any of	And when many terrible troubles come
their afflictions. Then	upon them,
this testimony will serve as evidence. . . ."	this song will confront them as a witness. . . ."

These examples illustrate very well how Jubilees uses the base text of Genesis and Exodus: it follows the narrative line closely, but does not quote the actual text itself extensively. Rather, it quotes short phrases and groups of verses, enough so that the base text is recognizable, but is interwoven that base text with extensive material from other books, in the form of quotation, but also, and more frequently, allusion. This is a type of harmonization, although it is less obviously so than the type we find in the pre-Samaritan group of texts. The result is a pastiche that uses "biblical" language throughout, but is transformed into a new composition. According to James C. VanderKam, the base text of Genesis and Exodus used by the composer of Jubilees was an independent text, not closely affiliated with any of the major witnesses, although it leans more toward the pre-Samaritan/Septuagint group than toward the proto-rabbinic text.[8]

Besides the other books of the Pentateuch, the composer of Jubilees used books that later became part of the Jewish canon. These books include the Former and Latter Prophets, Psalms, Chronicles, Ezra-Nehemiah, Job, and Ruth. Jubilees does not refer to these books by name or indicate that it is

8. VanderKam, *From Revelation to Canon*, 460.

quoting or alluding to them; this would destroy the fiction that the angel is dictating these words to Moses on Mount Sinai. Rather, the quotations or allusions are inserted without notice. For example, in a passage explaining why Abraham, although a model patriarch and righteous man, only lived to be 125 years of age, Jubilees inserts an allusion to Ps 90:10:

Jub 23:15	Ps 90:10
But now the days of our lives, if a man has lived for a long time, are seventy years and, if he is strong, eighty years. All are evil, and there is no peace. . . .	The days of our life are seventy years or perhaps eighty, if we are strong; even then their span is only toil and trouble; they are soon gone, and we fly away.

In addition to the works that later became canonical, Jubilees uses other Second Temple literature as source material. We have already seen in our discussion of 4QReworked Pentateuch (Chapter 3) that Jubilees preserves, in its Isaac-Rebekah cycle, a text very similar to one found in 4QReworked Pentateuch[b], that is, the farewell scene in which Rebekah mourns over the departure of Jacob (4Q364, frg. 3, col. ii; Jub 27:13-17). Whether Jubilees knows the text of 4QRP[b] or is simply drawing on the same tradition is not certain, but the similarity of the two passages demonstrates that the composer of Jubilees used a source rather than created something new here in this pericope.

Another Second Temple period work that the composer of Jubilees probably drew on is the Aramaic Levi Document, unearthed at Qumran. This work has been dated to the third century B.C.E., and is therefore older than Jubilees.[9] Aramaic Levi, as its name suggests, contains traditions concerning Levi and his elevation to the priesthood. Jubilees and Aramaic Levi share the following traditions: a version of the rape of Dinah and the destruction of Shechem (Genesis 34) that rehabilitates the actions of Levi; an angelic speech castigating exogamy (marriage to outsiders) and its consequences; a heavenly vision given to Levi, in which he is made a priest; a journey to visit Isaac, during which Isaac blesses Levi; and a scene at Bethel, in which Jacob tithes all his possessions and Levi first functions as a priest.[10] Since Aramaic Levi is older than Jubilees and was known in the same Jewish circles, as indicated by the presence of both in the Qumran caves, it seems safe to posit that Aramaic Levi served as a source for Jubilees.[11]

9. Greenfield, Stone, and Eshel, *The Aramaic Levi Document,* 19. I will use their system of chapter and verse for the Aramaic Levi Document throughout this chapter.

10. Kugler, *From Patriarch to Priest,* 147-49.

11. Also Stone, "Levi, Aramaic," 486.

Jubilees also demonstrates extensive familiarity with the books of Enoch and uses their traditions freely.[12] Jubilees knows at least three, and possibly four, of the five books that now make up 1 Enoch, but circulated separately in antiquity: the Astronomical Book (chs. 72–82), the Book of the Watchers (chs. 1–36), the Dream Visions (chs. 83–90), and possibly the Epistle (chs. 91–107). All of these books were composed by the early second century B.C.E., prior to Jubilees, and were part of the Qumran collection. The fifth book, the Parables (chs. 37–71), was probably composed later than Jubilees. The luni-solar calendar spelled out in the Astronomical Book of Enoch underlies the 364-day solar calendar of Jubilees, although Jubilees rejects the lunar aspect of Enoch's calendar: "The Lord appointed *the sun* as a great sign above the earth for days, sabbaths, months, festivals, years, sabbaths of years, jubilees, and all times of the years" (Jub 2:9; emphasis mine). Jubilees draws heavily on the Book of the Watchers in its retelling of the story of the misguided mating between the "sons of God" and the "daughters of men" found in Gen 6:1-4. However, Jubilees does not slavishly follow his Enochic source; where the Book of the Watchers depicts the descent of the angels to earth as wholly evil from its beginning, Jubilees portrays the initial descent of the angels as God's plan for the good of humanity: "During the second week of the tenth jubilee Malalael married Dinah, the daughter of Barakiel, the daughter of his father's brother. She gave birth to a son for him in the third week, in its sixth year. He named him Jared because during his lifetime the angels of the Lord who were called Watchers descended to earth to teach mankind and to do what is just and upright upon the earth" (Jub 4:15).[13] Thus the initial descent of the Watchers is for the good of humanity.

Jubilees also knows traditions about the figure of Enoch that are not found in the books of Enoch. Jub 4:23-26 has Enoch translated from earth to the garden of Eden; in 1 Enoch 70 he is translated into heaven.[14] We know that a variety of Enoch traditions existed in the Second Temple period, as the fragments of Pseudo-Eupolemos, a Samaritan writing in the second century B.C.E., attest. Jubilees is aware of these various traditions and uses them freely.

Jubilees' use of all of these books, both those that later became canonical and those that did not, testify to its broad and deep familiarity with Jewish literature available in the Second Temple period. The composer did not feel

---

12. VanderKam, *From Revelation to Canon*, 309-10.

13. Note the play on words with the Hebrew form of the name Jared; it comes from the root *y-r-d*, ירד, which means "to descend." The author of Jubilees uses the name as a "hook" to insert his story of the descent of the Watchers; VanderKam, "The Angel Story in the Book of Jubilees," 154-55.

14. VanderKam, *From Revelation to Canon*, 317.

himself constrained to cleave closely to his Genesis-Exodus text, as we find in both the pre-Samaritan group and in the Reworked Pentateuch group; rather, he uses it as a jumping-off point to bring together a wide variety of sources into a new and coherent whole. What was the purpose of his new composition? Why was Jubilees written?

Purpose of Jubilees

Jubilees retells the narrative of Genesis 1–Exodus 14 with particular polemical purposes. The composer uses his narrative mainly for what Geza Vermes termed "applied exegesis"; that is, he uses the story of Genesis and Exodus to demonstrate a particular point of the law or to illustrate a tenet that he wishes the reader to acknowledge. He does sometimes simply attempt to fill in gaps in the text or illuminate the text itself, which Vermes termed "pure exegesis."[15] For example, he supplies the names of the women who married the antediluvian ancestors. The name of Lamech's wife, the mother of Noah, is Betenos or Bitenosh (Jub 4:28), the same name that appears in the Genesis Apocryphon (see Chapter 6). But for the most part, the strategy of the author of Jubilees is to rewrite the text of Genesis-Exodus to illustrate the following themes:

1. Chronology and its corollary, calendar.
2. Law and ethics, especially matters of purity and (sexual) impurity. This theme includes the importance of Israel's separation from the Gentiles.
3. The elevation of Israel's ancestors as righteous examples, and the corresponding devaluation of those figures not among Israel's direct forebearers.
4. The priestly line descending from Noah through the patriarchs, culminating in the choice of Levi as priest.
5. Eschatology.[16]

Chronology

The chronology of the book of Jubilees is the most prominent theme in the book, and where it gets its title. The chronology is based on the 364-day solar calendar. Jubilees uses only the sun as the basis of its calendar: "The Lord appointed *the sun* as a great sign above the earth for days, sabbaths, months, fes-

---

15. See also Endres, *Biblical Interpretation in the Book of Jubilees*, 222.
16. See also Segal, *The Book of Jubilees*, 6-11, for a slightly different list.

tivals, years, sabbaths of years, jubilees, and all times of the years . . ." (Jub 2:9). According to Jubilees, this solar calendar is not a recent innovation, but was put in place by Noah after the Flood (6:17-38). Moreover, the use of the moon as a method for calculating the months is emphatically rejected.

> Now you command the Israelites to keep the years in this number — 364 days. Then the year will be complete and it will not disturb its time from its days or from its festivals because everything will happen in harmony with their testimony. They will neither omit a day nor disturb a festival. . . . There will be people who carefully observe the moon with lunar observations because it is corrupt (with respect to) the seasons and is early from year to year by ten days. Therefore years will come about for them when they will disturb (the year) and make a day of testimony something worthless and a profane day a festival. Everyone will join together both holy days with the profane and the profane day with the holy day, for they will err regarding the months, the sabbaths, the festivals, and the jubilee. (Jub 6:32, 36-37)

Thus Jubilees rejects not only the lunar calendar, in use among the Jews from at least the Babylonian Exile, but also the luni-solar calendar advocated by the books of Enoch and followed in the Qumran calendrical texts. Whether the 364-day solar calendar was actually used in its pure form anytime or anywhere in the Second Temple period is debated.[17]

Jubilees uses the 364-day solar calendar to construct an elaborate chronological system based on the number seven: years, weeks of years (seven years), and jubilees of years (forty-nine years). The idea of the jubilee period is based on Lev 25:8-12:

> You shall count off seven weeks of years, seven times seven years, so that the period of seven weeks of years gives forty-nine years. Then you shall have the trumpet sounded loud; on the tenth day of the seventh month — on the day of atonement — you shall have the trumpet sounded throughout all your land. And you shall hallow the fiftieth year and you shall proclaim liberty throughout all the land to all its inhabitants. It shall be a jubilee for you: you shall return, every one of you, to your property and every one of you to your family. That fiftieth year shall be a jubilee for you: you shall not sow, or reap the after growth, or harvest the unpruned vines. For it is a jubilee; it shall be holy to you: you shall eat only what the field itself produces.

17. VanderKam, *Calendars in the Dead Sea Scrolls*, 27-33.

However, in Leviticus the jubilee is the 50th year, following a period of 49 years; in Jubilees the jubilee is the 49-year period.[18] Thus the composer can give the date formula for any event and the reader can calculate the year since the foundation of the earth in which it occurred. For example, when Jacob arrives at Bethel for the first time (Gen 28:10-22), Jubilees gives the following date formula: "Jacob left the well of the oath to go to Haran during the first year of the second week of the forty-fourth jubilee. He arrived at Luz which is on the mountain — that is, Bethel — on the first of the first month of this week" (Jub 27:19). That is, 43 full jubilees have passed (2107 years), plus one entire week of years (seven years), and Jacob is now in the first year of the second week of years (one year). Thus, we find we are in the year 2115 from the creation of the world. This system allows the composer to calculate all dates (although his dates do not always agree with the more random system of Genesis-Exodus). All significant events can be dated according to this system, and particularly significant events have significant dates. For example, there will be 50 jubilees (a jubilee of jubilees) from the creation of the world until the entrance into the promised land, that is, 2450 years (Jub 50:4). The purpose of this elaborate chronology is to underscore the theological understanding that all of human history is foreordained, and is proceeding according to God's plan and with God's foreknowledge: "the Lord showed him what (had happened) beforehand as well as what was to come. He related to him the divisions of all the times — both of the law and of the testimony" (Jub 1:4).

This chronological system is not limited to Jubilees. It is found in 1 Enoch in the Apocalypse of Weeks (1 En 93, 91), in the later Testament of Levi, and in Dan 9:24-27, almost contemporary with Jubilees. Daniel, in fact, is using the system to reinterpret a passage in Jeremiah regarding the length of the exile:

> This whole land shall become a ruin and a waste, and these nations shall serve the king of Babylon seventy years. Then after seventy years are completed, I will punish the king of Babylon and that nation, the land of the Chaldeans, for their iniquity, says the LORD, making the land an everlasting waste. (Jer 25:11-12)

Daniel reinterprets Jeremiah as follows:

> Seventy weeks of years are decreed for your people and your holy city: to finish the transgression, to put an end to sin, and to atone for iniquity, to bring in everlasting righteousness, to seal both vision and prophet, and to

18. VanderKam, *From Revelation to Canon*, 524.

anoint a most holy place. Know therefore and understand: from the time that the word went out to restore and rebuild Jerusalem until the time of an anointed prince, there shall be seven weeks; and for sixty-two weeks, an anointed one shall be cut off and shall have nothing, and the troops of the prince who is to come shall destroy the city and the sanctuary. Its end shall come with a flood, and to the end there shall be war. Desolations are decreed. He shall make a strong covenant with many for one week, and for half of the week he shall make sacrifice and offering cease; and in their place shall be an abomination that desolates, until the decreed end is poured out upon the desolator. (Dan 9:24-27)

In Daniel, Jeremiah's 70 years becomes 70 weeks of years, and all the increments of time are calculated according to the formula "one week = seven years."

This system also appears in many Qumran texts, most notably those texts named pseudo-Moses and pseudo-Jeremiah, and in 11QMelchizedek.[19] So the chronological system that is the most striking feature of Jubilees was not an isolated phenomenon, but appears in several texts used by at least one group of Jews in the Second Temple period. We find it most fully developed in Jubilees.

Law and Ethics

The theme of law and ethics seeks to demonstrate that the law given to Moses at Sinai was not revealed for the first time there, but in fact had been known and practiced by the chosen ancestors of the Jews from the very beginning. Jubilees demonstrates that those items of the law which serve to separate Jews from the Gentiles, i.e., Sabbath observance, circumcision, avoidance of idolatry and the consumption of blood, and the prohibition of nakedness and intermarriage, were practiced by Israel's righteous ancestors. Thus there was no period of history in which the Jewish law was not valid, no period in which the Jews were not already a nation apart.[20] The purpose of this theme may have been to counteract the universalism that gained strength in the Hellenistic period, and particularly in the period when Jubilees was written, when a certain party of Jews wished to assimilate with the Gentile world (see, e.g., 1 Macc 1:11-13).

---

19. VanderKam, *From Revelation to Canon*, 525.
20. VanderKam, *The Book of Jubilees* (2001), 140.

Jubilees' treatment of the Sabbath commandment is a good illustration of this theme. The angel of the presence, who is dictating his text to Moses, informs him, in accordance with Gen 2:2-3, that God observed the first Sabbath by resting on the seventh day after creation: "He finished all his works on the sixth day. . . . He gave us the sabbath day as a great sign so that we should perform work for six days and that we should keep sabbath from all work on the seventh day" (Jub 2:16, 17). The base text of Genesis used by Jubilees states that God finished all the work of creation on the sixth day, in agreement with the Samaritan Pentateuch, the Septuagint, the Syriac, the Old Latin, and Josephus. This is against the reading of the Masoretic Text, which states that God finished all the work of creation on the seventh day. The latter reading creates an exegetical problem, for it could imply that God did work on the seventh day before he rested. Jubilees (or its base text) avoids the problem by having God finish the work on the sixth day.

According to Jubilees, it is not only God who rests on the seventh day after creation:

> He told us — all the angels of the presence and all the angels of holiness (these two great kinds) — to keep sabbath with him in heaven and on earth. He said to us: "I will now separate a people for myself from among my nations. They, too, will keep sabbath. I will sanctify the people for myself and will bless them as I sanctified the sabbath day. I will sanctify them for myself; in this way I will bless them. They will become my people and I will become their God. I have chosen the descendants of Jacob among all of those whom I have seen. . . . I will tell them about the sabbath days so that they may keep sabbath from all work on them." (Jub 2:18-20)

Thus, the Sabbath is both a divine and a heavenly ordinance, ordained since the beginning of time; further, God declared on that very first Sabbath his selection of Israel and their obligation to keep sabbath.

The importance of the Sabbath commandment is further emphasized by the fact that the angel of the presence reiterates it to Moses at the very end of the book (Jub 50:6-13). Thus the Sabbath commandment becomes an envelope that contains all the other commands in Jubilees. The penalty for desecrating the Sabbath is death (Jub 50:13); this accords with Exod 35:2: "Six days shall work be done, but on the seventh day you shall have a holy sabbath of solemn rest to the LORD; whoever does any work on it shall be put to death." Battle is forbidden on the Sabbath; that this was a problem for the Jews at the time of Jubilees' composition is illustrated by 1 Macc 2:29-38, in which the Hasideans are slaughtered on the Sabbath because of their refusal to fight. For this reason, the Maccabees decided to permit defensive fighting on the Sabbath (1 Macc 2:41), but Jubilees is uncompromising: "And any man who . . . makes war on the sabbath day — a man who does [this] on the sabbath day is to die" (Jub 50:12-13).

Sexual intercourse is likewise forbidden on the Sabbath (Jub 50:8). This may seem surprising, given that the later rabbis positively enjoined sexual intercourse on the Sabbath (*Ned.* 3.10; 8.6). However, there is some evidence from the Damascus Document that at least one group of Jews, the Essenes of which the Qumran community was a part, practiced a stricter asceticism by forbidding intercourse on the Sabbath (4QD^e 2 i 17-18).[21] The Karaites, almost certainly influenced by Essene practices, likewise forbade sexual intercourse on the Sabbath.

The observance of the Sabbath is a practice that separates Jews from Gentiles, and its emphasis serves the composer's purpose of demonstrating, through the narrative, that the Jews have been chosen, set apart, since the time of creation, and that any blurring of the line between Jews and Gentiles is an abrogation of the divine plan. The narrative treats other practices that separate Jews from Gentiles in the same way. Circumcision, according to Genesis 17, was first observed by Abraham. In Jubilees 15, Abraham is likewise the first human to practice circumcision. However, Jubilees expands the narrative of Genesis beyond the simple command that all males should be circumcised on the eighth day (Gen 17:10-14) with a sermonic elaboration that explains the reason for the commandment and the consequences for its abrogation (Jub 15:27-34). The text makes the rather startling declaration that the angels of the presence and the angels of sanctification were created circumcised; since God has sanctified Israel out of all humanity to be with him and his angels, they too are to be circumcised. Finally, the angel of the presence declares that there will come a time when the Israelites will not circumcise their sons; they will "treat their members like the Gentiles" (Jub 15:34). This is a situation that we know obtained during the Hellenistic reform and revolt of the mid-second century B.C.E.; according to 1 Macc 1:11-14,

> In those days certain renegades came out from Israel and misled many, saying, "Let us go and make a covenant with the Gentiles around us, for since we separated from them many disasters have come upon us." This proposal pleased them, and some of the people eagerly went to the king,

21. Crawford, "Not According to Rule," 134-35.

who authorized them to observe the ordinances of the Gentiles. So they built a gymnasium in Jerusalem, according to Gentile custom, and removed the marks of circumcision, and abandoned the holy covenant. They joined with the Gentiles and sold themselves to do evil.

It is probable that Jubilees' polemic is aimed against this situation. None of the changes introduced by Jubilees changes the essential narrative line of Genesis, but they do expand it and alter its emphasis, in keeping with the concerns of the composer.

Elevation of Israel's Ancestors

Jubilees also uses the technique of crediting Mosaic practices to the divinely chosen ancestors to bolster their antiquity and validity, as well as the righteousness of the ancestors. Thus, the various festivals and holy days celebrated by the Israelites, e.g., the festivals of Weeks and Sukkoth and the holy day of Yom Kippur, were not instituted by Moses, but already practiced by the righteous patriarchs. The author of Jubilees uses the narrative of Genesis to make this legal point. So, for example, when Noah exits the ark in Genesis, he makes a sacrifice; as a result God makes a covenant with Noah and his sons, the sign of which is the rainbow (Gen 8:20–9:17). In Jubilees 6 those events take place in that order; but Noah's sacrifice is an atoning sacrifice, for which he offers the proper animals in the proper manner, salted and with incense. God then makes a covenant with Noah and his sons, the sign of which is the rainbow. But in Jubilees this covenant is the reason for the celebration of the Feast of Weeks, which according to Jubilees' chronology falls at the time Noah leaves the ark (the third month). According to Jubilees, the Feast of Weeks was celebrated by the angels in heaven until the time of Noah, by Noah and his sons until Noah's death, then by Abraham, Isaac, and Jacob and his sons; it is now being reinstituted in the time of Moses (Jub 6:18-19). So a Mosaic festival is retrojected by Jubilees back to a divine ancestor.

Likewise, it is the righteous Abraham who first celebrates the festival of Sukkoth (Booths), at the time when Sarah is found to be pregnant (Jub 16:10-31). Jacob is the patriarch who first observes Yom Kippur, a passage that demonstrates the composer's exegetical skill. Jubilees follows the narrative of Genesis 37, in which Jacob sends Joseph out to his brothers, his brothers plot at first to slay him but instead sell him to Ishmaelite merchants, and then deceive their father into thinking that Joseph is dead by soaking his coat in goat's blood (Jub 34:10-12). However, Jubilees, as is its wont, supplies a date scheme for these events, so that Jacob receives Joseph's coat on the tenth day of the seventh month, the date of Yom Kippur (Lev 23:26). Thus the Day of Atonement is ordained as a commemoration of Jacob's mourning for Joseph, and the sacrifice of a goat is commanded (Num 29:11) because Joseph's coat was dipped in goat's blood. So Jubilees uses the seemingly incidental aspects of the Genesis narrative (Jacob's mourning, the goat's blood) to retroject the holy day of Yom Kippur back into the patriarchal period.

Although we have been discussing the book of Jubilees' practice of expanding the Genesis-Exodus narrative by various means in order to make its own exegetical points, Jubilees also omits things from the Genesis-Exodus narrative if they are not in keeping with its themes or are extraneous to its purposes. This practice is most visible in Jubilees' treatment of the patriarchal narratives. Since Jubilees wishes to portray Israel's ancestors as completely righteous, keeping the festivals and observing the law, the peccadilloes of those same ancestors, which are portrayed in such lively tones in Genesis, run contrary to its purpose. For example, in Gen 12:10-20 Abram goes down to Egypt, where he instructs Sarai to say that she is his sister, not his wife. The result is that Sarai is taken into Pharaoh's harem, where her sexual integrity is obviously compromised; she must be rescued from this situation by God himself. The Genesis narrative throws Abram's integrity into question; is he more interested in saving his own skin than in protecting his wife? Jubilees handles this problem by eliminating the element of deception altogether: "When the pharaoh took Abram's wife Sarai by force for himself, the Lord punished the pharaoh and his household very severely because of Abram's wife Sarai" (Jub 13:13). Abram cannot be at fault if Pharaoh simply "took" Sarai "by force." Thus a potential blot on Abram's character is removed. Isaac and Jacob are likewise portrayed as exceptionally righteous and ethical, and any hint to the contrary is scrupulously omitted. Rebekah, already arguably the most prominent female character in Genesis, becomes in Jubilees the model matriarch; her every action indicates her God-given wisdom and righteousness.[22]

A more neutral example of omission occurs in the Noah story. In Gen 6:13-22 God gives Noah instructions for building and stocking the ark in preparation for the Flood. Jubilees omits all the particulars of this passage, simply summarizing with "He ordered Noah to make himself an ark in order to save himself from the flood waters. Noah made an ark in every respect as he had ordered him . . ." (Jub 5:21-22). Jubilees shortens the Genesis text here because the information it contains is extraneous to its main purpose. This

---

22. Halpern-Amaru, *The Empowerment of Women in the Book of Jubilees.*

omission is also a clue that the composer does not intend his work to be a substitute for Genesis; he does not feel the need to repeat every scrap of the Genesis narrative, for presumably it would be available to his readers in Genesis itself.

The Levitical Priestly Line

Another major theme in the book of Jubilees is the descent of the priestly line from Noah through the patriarchs, culminating in the elevation of Levi to the priesthood. Noah is the first of Israel's ancestors to offer a proper atoning sacrifice, after the Flood:

> On the first of the third month he left the ark and built an altar on this mountain. He appeared on the earth, took a kid, and atoned with its blood for all the sins of the earth because everything that was on it had been obliterated except those who were in the ark with Noah. He placed the fat on the altar. Then he took a bull, a ram, a sheep, goats, salt, a turtledove, and a dove and offered (them as) a burnt offering on the altar. He poured on them an offering mixed with oil, sprinkled wine, and put frankincense on everything. He sent up a pleasant fragrance that was pleasing before the Lord. (Jub 6:1-3)

This is the first celebration, according to Jubilees, of the Feast of Weeks (Jub 6:17-18). Abraham likewise functions as a priest, celebrating the Feast of Weeks and the Feast of Sukkoth (Booths) (chs. 15, 16, 22). Abraham also gives Isaac detailed instructions for the proper offering of sacrifices (21:7-17). Jacob, however, does not function as a priest; that honor is reserved for his third son, Levi.[23]

Levi is hardly an important character in Genesis, and certainly there is no inkling of the later prominence of his tribe. There is a notice about his birth (Gen 29:34), and he appears in the various lists of Jacob's sons found in Genesis (35:22-26; 46:8-27). Otherwise, in the only narrative that features Levi he acts with his brother Simeon to avenge the defilement of their sister Dinah by Shechem, an act that is not greeted with approbation by Jacob (Gen 34:25-31). In fact, in Jacob's (non)blessing in Gen 49:5-7, he says concerning Levi (and Simeon):

23. This is the same line of priestly descent found in Aramaic Levi; Greenfield, Stone, and Eshel, *The Aramaic Levi Document,* 36.

Simeon and Levi are brothers; weapons of violence are their swords. May I never come into their council; may I not be joined to their company — for in their anger they killed men, and at their whim they hamstrung oxen. Cursed be their anger, for it is fierce, and their wrath, for it is cruel! I will divide them in Jacob, and scatter them in Israel.

It is difficult to understand from the Genesis narrative how the descendants of Levi could have become the priestly tribe of Israel. It is therefore the exegetical task of the composer of Jubilees to rehabilitate Levi.[24]

He begins his task in his retelling of the incident of Dinah and Shechem (Jub 30). He adds the information that Dinah was only 12 years old when Shechem carried her off, which makes the crime worse. He then signals his approval of the slaughter by Simeon and Levi with a sermonic elaboration that polemicizes against intermarriage with Gentiles. He praises Simeon, and especially Levi, for their actions:

Proclaim this testimony to Israel: "See how it turned out for the Shechemites and their children — how they were handed over to Jacob's two sons. They killed them in a painful way. It was a just act for them and was recorded as a just act for them." Levi's descendants were chosen for the priesthood and as Levites to serve before the Lord as we do for all time. Levi and his sons will be blessed forever because he was zealous to carry out justice, punishment, and revenge on all who rise against Israel. (Jub 30:17-18)

The word "zealous" marks an allusion to the story of Phinehas, the grandson of Aaron, who slew an Israelite man for having sexual intercourse with a Midianite woman, also a crime of intermarriage (Num 25:6-9).[25] For his action Phinehas is rewarded with a covenant of perpetual priesthood:

The LORD spoke to Moses, saying: "Phinehas son of Eleazar, son of Aaron the priest, has turned back my wrath from the Israelites by manifesting such *zeal* among them on my behalf that in my jealousy I did not consume the Israelites. Therefore say, 'I hereby grant him my covenant of peace. It shall be for him and for his descendants after him a covenant of perpetual priesthood, because he was *zealous* for his God, and made atonement for the Israelites.'" (Num 25:10-13; emphasis mine)

24. As noted above, the author draws on the Aramaic Levi Document for much of his material in this section. See Greenfield, Stone, and Eshel, *The Aramaic Levi Document*, 35-41.

25. It is of interest to note that the man in question was a member of the tribe of Simeon.

Likewise in Jubilees Levi is rewarded with a covenant of eternal priesthood (Jub 30:18). Thus Jubilees turns the Genesis story upside down; what was worthy of condemnation has become laudatory.

Next, in ch. 31, Jacob returns to his father Isaac, bringing with him his sons Levi and Judah. Isaac blesses both boys, with Levi receiving pride of place on his right side. Isaac blesses Levi first as a priest, and says to him,

> "May the Lord of everything — he is the Lord of all ages — bless you and your sons throughout all ages. May the Lord give you and your descendants extremely great honor; may he make you and your descendants (alone) out of all humanity approach him to serve in his temple like the angels of the presence and like the holy ones." (Jub 31:13-14)

This scene has no equivalent in the text of Genesis; however, it is a clear allusion to another scene in Gen 48:11-22, in which Jacob blesses Ephraim and Manasseh, giving Ephraim (in this case the younger son) pride of place on his right side. As does Jacob, so does Isaac in Jubilees. We have already noted that the Aramaic Levi Document, a probable source for Jubilees, also says that Isaac blesses Levi.[26] It is striking that Isaac's blessing of Levi and Judah in Jubilees gives Levi, the priestly ancestor, pride of place over Judah, the royal ancestor. This motif ties Jubilees even more closely to the thought of the Qumran Essenes, who, especially in their messianic expectations, consistently elevated the priesthood over the kingship (see, e.g., the Rule of the Congregation [1QSa], col. 2). As we shall see, the Temple Scroll also subordinates the monarchy to the priesthood.

Finally, in ch. 32, Levi has a dream at Bethel that he has been made a priest. Bethel is the place where God declares his choice of Jacob in a dream (Gen 28:10-17), so it is apt as a location for Levi's dream. This tradition that Levi receives a prescient dream is also known from the Aramaic Levi Document (Aramaic Levi Document 4:4-13), and in the later Testament of Levi (*T. Levi* 2:6–5:7). The next morning Jacob gives a tithe of all his possessions to the Lord; in a neat bit of exegesis, the composer of Jubilees has Jacob count his sons from the youngest up, beginning with Benjamin, still in the womb. Counting upwards in this way the 10th son is Levi (he is the third oldest), who becomes Jacob's tithe to the Lord. Jacob both tithes Levi to God and tithes to Levi as a priest. This recalls the scene in Gen 14:17-20, in which Abram tithes to Melchizedek, the priest-king of Salem, the only character given the title "priest" in the book of Genesis (with the exception of Egyptian priests in the

---

26. Aramaic Levi Document, 5:6-8. Greenfield, Stone, and Eshel, *The Aramaic Levi Document*, 70-71.

Joseph cycle). Thus, although the scene in Jubilees (which also appears in Aramaic Levi Document 5:1-5) has no equivalent in the book of Genesis, it is anchored in the Genesis narrative by means of allusion.

Jubilees emphasizes God's choice of Levi for the priesthood by a variety of exegetical techniques: Levi is rehabilitated in the Shechem episode, he is blessed by Isaac, he has a prescient dream, and he becomes a tithe to the Lord. There can be no doubt as to Levi's status as a priest, according to the understanding of the priestly office in the Torah. But for Jubilees there is more to the office of priest than the proper functioning of the cult, as important as that is. In Jubilees, the priestly line, starting with Noah, is the keeper of a scribal tradition that emphasizes the study and observance of the law and the preservation of the tradition in written form. The tradition is preserved in books, passed down from ancestor to ancestor. The tradition actually begins with Enoch before the Flood. Enoch is credited with being the first to learn "writing, instruction, and wisdom" (Jub 4:17). Enoch writes down everything he witnesses and learns, both on earth and with the angels (4:17-19, 21-22). It is this esoteric, scribal knowledge, in the form of books, which is passed down through the priestly line. Noah receives his traditions from his forefathers, Enoch, Methusaleh, and Lamech (7:38); after the Flood he writes down everything and gives it to Shem (10:14). Abraham studies his father's books in Hebrew (12:27). Jacob, the righteous ancestor, learns writing, but Esau does not (19:14). Finally, Jacob gives all his books to his son Levi, the priest (45:15).[27] Thus the priests are to be the keepers of the written, scribal tradition of interpretation, which is enshrined in the book of Jubilees itself.[28] That this written tradition is divinely inspired is emphasized by the fact that much of it is recorded on the "heavenly tablets." These "heavenly tablets" also appear in the Enoch literature.[29] The heavenly tablets contain all the law that is revealed to Moses on the mountain (1:29), but especially those specific laws of particular interest to the author (e.g., the law of circumcision, 15:26), and information about important figures such as Abraham, about whom it says that he was "recorded on the heavenly tablets as the friend of the Lord" (19:9). So the existence of these heavenly tablets and the revelation of their contents in the written tradition preserved in Jubilees is further evidence of Jubilees' divine authority.

27. Aramaic Levi also credits Levi with reading and writing and emphasizes the priest's role as scribe and sage; Kugler, *From Patriarch to Priest,* 129; Greenfield, Stone, and Eshel, *The Aramaic Levi Document,* 34-38.

28. VanderKam, *The Book of Jubilees* (2001), 118-20.

29. VanderKam, *The Book of Jubilees* (2001), 89. For a full discussion of the "Heavenly Tablats," see García Martínez, "The Heavenly Tablets in the Book of Jubilees."

Eschatology

The last major theme of the book of Jubilees is eschatology in the form of predictive history. It is with this theme that Jubilees departs most radically from its Genesis-Exodus base text. This theme begins in ch. 1, in which God, speaking to Moses on Mount Sinai, foretells Israel's apostasy and final redemption (Jub 1:7-18). The eschatological interest of the composer of Jubilees, who evidently believed the end times were rapidly approaching, is revealed in the last verse of ch. 1:

> The angel of the presence, who was going along in front of the Israelite camp, took the tablets (which told) of the divisions of the years from the time the law and the testimony were created — for the weeks of their jubilees, year by year in their full number, and their jubilees from [the time of the creation until] the time of the new creation when the heavens, the earth, and all their creatures will be renewed like the powers of the sky and like all the creatures of the earth, until the time when the temple of the Lord will be created in Jerusalem on Mt. Zion. (Jub 1:29)

Other large interpolations that contain predictive history occur throughout Jubilees, in the story of Noah (Jub 7:34-38), and Abraham (15:31-34), but especially in ch. 23, which has been sometimes labeled a little apocalypse. In it the angel of the presence predicts the rise of an evil generation, which brings about war, the destruction of the land, and the defilement of the temple (23:14-22). This is probably a reference to the desecration of the temple in the time of Antiochus Epiphanes (Dan 9:27; 1 Macc 1:54). At that point the author leaves what we can identify as historical events and moves into future prediction, which gives a good indication of Jubilees' date of composition.

> They will cause chaos in Israel and sin against Jacob. Much blood will be shed on the earth, and there will be no one who gathers up (corpses) or who buries (them). At that time they will cry out and call and pray to be rescued from the power of the sinful nations, but there will be no one who rescues (them). The children's heads will turn white with gray hair. A child who is three weeks of age will look old like one whose years are 100, and their condition will be destroyed through distress and pain. In those days the children will begin to study the laws, to seek out the commands, and to return to the right way. The days will begin to become numerous and increase, and mankind as well — generation by generation and day by day until their lifetimes approach 1000 years and to more years than the number of days (had been). There will be no old man, nor

anyone who has lived out his lifetime, because all of them will be infants and children. They will be complete and live their entire lifetimes peacefully and joyfully. There will be neither a satan nor any evil one who will destroy. For their entire lifetimes will be times of blessing and healing. (Jub 23:23-29)

The nadir of human history is marked by violence and bloodshed and the shortness of the human life span. The upward or redemptive trend begins when "the children begin to study the laws, to seek out the commands and to return to the right way" — in other words, when the tradition enshrined in Jubilees is rediscovered and followed.

None of these passages of predictive history is tied closely to the Genesis-Exodus narrative, although they contain countless allusions to other books available in the Second Temple period. This theme of eschatology and predictive history is one that clearly marks Jubilees as a new composition, separate from Genesis-Exodus and meant to stand on its own. It also reinforces the book's claim to divine authority, since it is God and the angel of the presence who are foretelling this history to Moses.

Conclusion

We have demonstrated how Jubilees has used its base text of Genesis-Exodus to create a new work, one that illustrated the major themes it wished to emphasize. Those themes either were not present in the text of Genesis-Exodus (the chronology based on the solar year, eschatology), were there only by implication (law and ethics as practiced by the divinely chosen ancestors, separation of Israel from the nations), or had to be achieved through exegetical manipulation of the base text (elevation of Levi to the priesthood). To create his new composition the composer used verbatim quotation of his base text, harmonization, paraphrase, paraphrase of or allusion to Scripture or other Second Temple works, and the addition of new material, in particular sermonic elaborations and the importation of legal commentary into a narrative text. What was the purpose of this new composition? What status did the composer hope the book would achieve among its readers?

He is clearly claiming divine authority for the book of Jubilees. The setting is Mount Sinai, the recipient is Moses, the authority is God, and the conduit is an angel of the presence.[30] If anyone questioned the book's authority,

30. Najman, *Seconding Sinai*, 43-69.

the answer was evident from the book itself: did it not accurately predict the downfall and apostasy of the Israelites, as evidenced by contemporary events?

Jubilees belongs, we have demonstrated above, in the line of tradition in which interpretation of Scripture was a written activity.[31] In fact, Jubilees is the first text we have studied that openly embraces this line of tradition, by claiming to be part of a written tradition that goes back as far as Enoch. This line of interpretation is demonstrated in its most conservative manifestation in the harmonizing activity observed in the pre-Samaritan texts, which emphasize the "perfection" of the scriptural text. It continues in the "hyper-expansiveness" of the Reworked Pentateuch group, which begins to add material from elsewhere in the interpretive tradition into the scriptural text, and now moves into the creation of new written compositions based on the received text, as we see in Jubilees. The texts of the first two groups are not copies of one another (although obviously copies could be, and were, made of individual texts); each scribe was free, within the bounds of the tradition, to work with his text individually. The composer of Jubilees has fully utilized the freedom of this tradition to create a new work. This is a line of tradition that differs sharply from the later rabbinic view of scripture, in which an Oral Torah was given to Moses at Sinai alongside the written one. The written text, in this latter tradition, remains relatively unchanged (allowing for normal scribal error). We may see this line of tradition forming in the proto-rabbinic group of texts, already in existence in the late Second Temple period. In any case, Jubilees belongs to the first line of tradition, in which a written authority is claimed, and the received text is open to change.

But was this new written composition, Jubilees, meant to supercede its base text of Genesis-Exodus, or even the entire Torah? Evidently not. Jubilees, first, assumes the existence of the second half of Exodus and the whole of Leviticus, Numbers, and Deuteronomy by its extensive use of those books in its retelling of the Genesis narrative. However, it leaves much in these books unsaid and unused and refers in several places to the "First Law," evidently the Torah. Therefore it is clear that Jubilees assumes that the "First Law," received by Moses on Mount Sinai at the same time as Jubilees, continues to be valid and authoritative. Second, it does not appear as if Jubilees is meant to supercede Genesis and the first half of Exodus either. As we noted above, the composer of Jubilees omits information from his base text that is extraneous to his main purpose, such as God's instructions to Noah concerning the ark. That information was still accessible in the received text of Genesis. Jubilees was certainly meant, however, to be read alongside Genesis-Exodus, to ex-

31. See also Najman, *Seconding Sinai*, 62-63.

plain away problems in that text, and to be accepted as an equal, if not greater, authority.

Did it achieve that divine, authoritative status among any group in Second Temple Judaism? The evidence from Qumran points to the fact that among the Essenes, for whom Qumran was a major center, it did. There were 14 or 15 copies of Jubilees preserved at Qumran, more than for most of the books that later became canonical. It was cited as an authoritative text by the Damascus Document, one of the key documents of the Essene movement, also found in multiple copies at Qumran. Its chronology, based on a system of counting by jubilees, surfaces in a number of documents from Qumran (although at Qumran the luni-solar calendar of Enoch would appear to be in favor).[32] All of these indicators point to the fact that Jubilees had a divine authoritative status in the Essene community centered at Qumran. Further, Jubilees belongs to a constellation of texts, including the books of Enoch and the Aramaic Levi Document, whose priestly-levitical ideas and traditions enjoy a special prominence in the Qumran library, resurfacing again and again in the texts discovered in the Qumran caves.

It would also appear that in the early Christian movement Jubilees was an esteemed book, as evidenced by its translation into Greek, Latin, and Syriac. It was also quoted fairly extensively by the early church fathers. However, it did not become canonical in either the Eastern or Western church, and it does not seem to have been an object of canonical debate. The sole exception to this was the Abyssinian Orthodox Church, which included Jubilees in its canon and preserved it in its entirety in Ethiopic.

BIBLIOGRAPHY

Crawford, Sidnie White. "Not According to Rule: Women, the Dead Sea Scrolls and Qumran." In *Emanuel: Studies in Hebrew Bible, Septuagint, and Dead Sea Scrolls in Honor of Emanuel Tov,* ed. Shalom M. Paul, Robert A. Kraft, Lawrence H. Schiffman, and Weston W. Fields, 127-50. VTSup 94. Leiden: Brill, 2003.

Endres, John C. *Biblical Interpretation in the Book of Jubilees.* CBQMS 18. Washington: Catholic Biblical Association, 1987.

García Martínez, Florentino. "The Heavenly Tablets in the Book of Jubilees." In *Studies in the Book of Jubilees,* ed. M. Albani, J. Frey, and A. Lange, 333-349. TSAJ 65. Tübingen: J. C. B. Mohr, 1997.

32. VanderKam, *Calendars in the Dead Sea Scrolls,* 74.

Greenfield, Jonas C., Michael E. Stone, and Esther Eshel. *The Aramaic Levi Document: Edition, Translation, Commentary.* SVTP 19. Leiden: Brill, 2004.

Halpern-Amaru, Betsy. *The Empowerment of Women in the Book of Jubilees.* SJSJ 60. Leiden: Brill, 1999.

Kugler, Robert A. *From Patriarch to Priest: The Levi-Priestly Tradition from Aramaic Levi to Testament of Levi.* SBLEJL 9. Atlanta: Scholars, 1996.

Najman, Hindy. *Seconding Sinai: The Development of Mosaic Discourse in Second Temple Judaism.* SJSJ 77. Leiden: Brill, 2003.

Segal, Michael. *The Book of Jubilees: Rewritten Bible, Redaction, Ideology and Theology.* SJSJ 117. Leiden: Brill, 2007.

Stone, Michael E. "Levi, Aramaic." In *EDSS,* 1:486-88.

VanderKam, James C. "The Angel Story in the Book of Jubilees." In *Pseudepigraphic Perspectives: The Apocrypha and Pseudepigrapha in Light of the Dead Sea Scrolls,* ed. Esther Chazon and Michael E. Stone, 151-70. STDJ 31. Leiden: Brill, 1999.

———. *The Book of Jubilees: A Critical Text.* 2 vols. CSCO 510-11. Scriptores Aethiopici 87-88. Louvain: Peeters, 1989.

———. *The Book of Jubilees.* Guides to Apocrypha and Pseudepigrapha. Sheffield: Sheffield Academic, 2001.

———. *Calendars in the Dead Sea Scrolls: Measuring Time.* London: Routledge, 1998.

———. *From Revelation to Canon: Studies in the Hebrew Bible and Second Temple Judaism.* SJSJ 62. Leiden: Brill, 2000.

———, and J. T. Milik. "Jubilees." In *Qumran Cave 4.VIII: Parabiblical Texts, Part 1,* ed. Harold Attridge, T. Elgvin, *et al.,* 1-186. DJD 13. Oxford: Clarendon, 1994.

CHAPTER 5

The Temple Scroll

The Temple Scroll is one of the new, previously unknown compositions to emerge from the Qumran caves. It exists in at least three, and possibly four, copies, although none of these copies is an exact replica of another.

Description of the Manuscripts

The largest and best-known manuscript of the Temple Scroll is 11QTemple[a], discovered in Cave 11 and first published by Yigael Yadin in 1977 (Hebrew; rev. Eng. ed. 1983). This scroll is the longest surviving manuscript from the Qumran caves, composed of 19 sheets of leather for a total length of 8.148 meters. Seven of its sheets contain three inscribed columns, while 10 sheets contain four columns. The last sheet, a "handle sheet," is completely blank. Sheets 2-18 were copied by a single scribe, whose hand dates paleographically to between 25 B.C.E. and 25 C.E. Sheet 1, which contains five columns, was copied by a second scribe whose dates are slightly later. We can assume that sheet no. 1 was a replacement sheet for a damaged original, indicating much use and consequent wear. 11QTemple[a], as the most complete exemplar of the Temple Scroll, is the manuscript against which all other copies are compared and will be the default manuscript in this discussion of the Temple Scroll, unless otherwise specified.

Cave 11 yielded another copy of the Temple Scroll, 11QTemple[b].[1] It dates to approximately 20-50 C.E. and was copied by the same scribe as 1QPesher

---

1. García Martínez, Tigchelaar, and van der Woude, "11QTemple[b]."

Habakkuk. Although fragmentary, the manuscript covers almost all of 11QTemple[a], and its corrections (in a different hand) were made according to 11QTemple[a]. According to its editors, the preserved fragments of 11QTemple[b] show "few, if any, differences" from 11QTemple[a].[2]

A possible third copy of the Temple Scroll, 11QTemple[c?], was found in Cave 11.[3] The manuscript preserves only three fragments, with a paleographic date of *ca.* 50 C.E. It is possible that its scribe was the same as the scribe who copied 11QJubilees. Fragment 1 may contain an overlap with 11QTemple[a], while fragments 2 and 3 do not contain overlaps. However, Elisha Qimron locates fragment 3 at the beginning of column 48 in his reconstruction of the Temple Scroll.[4]

A most important copy of the Temple Scroll was recovered from Cave 4. 4QRouleau du Temple (4Q524) dates to 150-125 B.C.E., before the founding of the Qumran community. Its editor states that it must be a copy since it contains corrections.[5] 4QRT contains overlaps with 11QTemple[a], almost entirely in the latter's last 17 columns, and one overlap with 11QTemple[b]. However, 4QRT continues beyond the ending of 11QTemple[a] (col. 67), indicating that it contains a different (and older) form of the Temple Scroll.

Finally, a small manuscript from Cave 4, 4Q365a, may contain source material for the Temple Scroll. The manuscript, which dates to *ca.* 75-50 B.C.E., has one fragment with inexact parallels to the Temple Scroll and four other fragments with similar content.[6] This manuscript may give concrete evidence for the theory that the author/redactor of the Temple Scroll used sources to produce his composition.

Category

I have placed the Temple Scroll in the Rewritten Scripture category at the point along the spectrum occupied by new works that are still recognizably tied to their scriptural base text and claim the same authority as that base text. This is the position also occupied by Jubilees, which is chiefly a narrative work. Both works are also pseudepigraphs; Jubilees, as we have seen, claims to have been dictated to Moses on Mount Sinai by an angel of the presence. The Temple Scroll is a more audacious pseudepigraph: it claims to have been spo-

---

2. García Martínez, Tigchelaar, and van der Woude, "11QTemple[b]," 365.

3. García Martínez, Tigchelaar, and van der Woude, "11QTemple[c?]."

4. Qimron, *The Temple Scroll*, 69.

5. Puech, "4QRouleau du Temple," 88.

6. White (Crawford), "4QTemple?"; Crawford, "Three Fragments from Qumran Cave 4."

ken by God, in the first person, directly, to Moses on Mount Sinai! This is demonstrated by the change from third person found in its base text to first person throughout the Scroll (although the author/redactor is inconsistent), e.g., col. 55:11-14: ". . . that I may turn from the fierceness of my anger, and show you mercy, and have compassion on you, and multiply you, as I swore to your fathers, if you obey my voice, keeping all my commandments which I command you this day, and doing what is right and good in the sight of the Lord your God." The base text for this passage is Deut 13:18b-19, which is couched in the third person: ". . . in order that the LORD your God may turn from his anger and show you mercy and have compassion on you and multiply you, as he swore to your fathers: if you obey the voice of the LORD your God, obeying all his commandments which I [Moses] am commanding today, doing what is right in the sight of the LORD your God." This pseudepigraphic conceit makes the Temple Scroll's claim to authority uncontestable: since God is speaking directly, the legal regulations set down in the Scroll are by their very nature definitive and unalterable.[7] The author/redactor's device carries the claim to authority made by all pseudepigraphic texts to its logical extreme. Whether or not that claim to authority was validated by community acceptance will be discussed below.

The Temple Scroll thus shares two major characteristics with the book of Jubilees: they have both departed from their pentateuchal base texts far enough to be termed separate works (unlike, e.g., Reworked Pentateuch), and they are both pseudepigraphs set during the revelation to Moses on Mount Sinai. The Temple Scroll differs from Jubilees, however, by being a *sepher torah*, a book of the Law. The entire focus of the Temple Scroll is on legal matters; it contains almost no narrative material.[8] My argument that the Temple Scroll belongs in the category Rewritten Scripture thus pushes the bounds of that definition beyond that given by Geza Vermes.[9] I think it is legitimate to do that, however, since the author/redactor of the Temple Scroll uses the same techniques found in the narrative texts to demonstrate that the extrapentateuchal legislation that he embraces was also given by God to Moses at the time of the Sinaitic revelation. That is, he assimilates, by techniques of conflation, harmonization, modifications, additions for clarification, and addition through exegesis, those extrapentateuchal traditions into a new Book of the Law. He also follows in his broad outline for the work the

7. Milgrom, "The Qumran Cult," 178.

8. The introduction to the Scroll (cols. [1]-2) may have contained some narrative material at its beginning, in order to set the scene, but the context is very broken.

9. See also Bernstein, "'Rewritten Bible,'" 194-95.

order of the canonical Torah, beginning with Exodus 34 and ending with Deuteronomy 23, although within the body of the text he moves around from book to book.[10]

The legal interests of the author/redactor of the Temple Scroll are not all encompassing. He concentrates on matters of cult, especially the physical temple and its furnishings, the proper sacrifices, the role of the Levites, the Festival Calendar, and issues of purity and impurity, as well as the rights and duties of kingship and certain regulations concerning daily life in the land. He thus constructs a picture of an ideal Israel as a worshipping community with a gigantic temple as both its physical and spiritual center. These interests indicate that these were most likely areas of controversy when he did his work; they are also the concerns we have enumerated before for the priestly-levitical tradition of interpretation and exegesis we have been tracing. The author/redactor does not, however, attempt to replace the already-existing Torah (as argued by Ben Zion Wacholder[11]), which he clearly considers legitimate and divinely inspired. The Temple Scroll is meant to stand alongside the Torah, to supplement and explain it, as, in similar fashion and for similar reasons, is the book of Jubilees.[12]

Authoritative Status

Whether or not the Temple Scroll was accepted by a community as an authoritative text, as was clearly intended by its author/redactor, remains an open question. Recall the criteria for judging a Qumran text as authoritative we have set out before: the work should present itself as authoritative; the work may be quoted or alluded to as an authority and/or the work may be the subject of a commentary; and it may exist in multiple copies (evidence that the community considered it important enough to keep many copies). The Temple Scroll only meets with certainty the first of these criteria. It is never clearly quoted or alluded to as an authority, as Jubilees is; therefore it does not meet the strongest criterion for scriptural status. However, it does share a general theological/legal stance we have called priestly-levitical in common with other texts that were almost certainly authoritative to at least certain groups of Jews in the Second Temple period, including the Essene movement of

---

10. This is another indication that the order of the books of the Pentateuch was accepted as fixed in the Second Temple period.

11. Wacholder, *The Dawn of Qumran.*

12. Najman, *Seconding Sinai*, 47.

which the Qumran community was a part: 1 Enoch, Jubilees, Aramaic Levi, and the Damascus Document.[13] Thus, it is possible but uncertain if the Temple Scroll enjoyed an authoritative status at any time in its existence as a living text.[14]

Date and Provenance

The question of the date and provenance of the Temple Scroll may be fixed within certain limits. The existence of 4QRouleau du Temple, which its editor dates to *ca.* 150-125 B.C.E.,[15] sheds some light on the question. If, as Émile Puech argues, 4QRT is not a source for the Temple Scroll but an actual copy of it, the author/redactor must have worked prior to 150 B.C.E. This is prior to the founding of the Qumran community.[16] Thus the Temple Scroll is a pre-Qumranic document, preserved in the form found in the Cave 4 copy by the community because of its affinities with the ideology of the sect. That is, the Temple Scroll, like 1 Enoch, Jubilees, and the Aramaic Levi Document, belongs to a constellation of texts that seem to have originated within priestly-levitical circles in the Second Temple period and were inherited by the Qumran community.[17]

In the first 75 years of its existence, however, the community did not seem to take much interest in the Temple Scroll. That seems to have changed in the latter stages of the community's life, when the Temple Scroll was copied at least twice (11QTemple[a&b]) and probably edited into the form we find in 11QTemple[a]. This upsurge of interest may have been brought about by contemporary events: the excesses of the Hasmonaean and Herodian kings, the ascendancy of the Pharisees in matters of cult and purity regulations and the subsequent sharpening of their conflict with the Qumran Essenes, and above all the rebuilding of the temple by Herod. All of these events sparked a renewal of interest in the old program for the ideal temple and community found in the Temple Scroll.

---

13. Najman, *Seconding Sinai*, 59, points out that the Temple Scroll lacks the emphasis on the "writtenness" of its tradition that is found in other works in this group.

14. Here I disagree with VanderKam and Flint, who place the Temple Scroll in their "certain" category; *The Meaning of the Dead Sea Scrolls*, 178.

15. Puech, "4QRouleau du Temple," 87.

16. Magness, *The Archaeology of Qumran and the Dead Sea Scrolls*, 66-69.

17. Brooke, "The Textual Tradition of the Temple Scroll," 282; Mink, "The Use of Scripture in the Temple Scroll," 28.

Description of the Contents

From the time of its first publication, the Temple Scroll has been recognized as a composite document, containing sources which a redactor skillfully wove together to create a unified whole.[18] In an early article, Andrew Wilson and Lawrence Wills[19] identified five sources in 11QTemple[a]: (1) a Temple and Courts source (cols. 2:1–13:8, 30:3–47:18); (2) a calendar source (cols. 13:9–30:2); (3) the purity laws (cols. 48:1–51:10); (4) the laws of polity (cols. 51:11–56:21, 60:1–66:7); (5) the Torah of the King (cols. 57-59). In 1990 Michael Wise attempted to revise and refine their theory by positing the presence of four major sources: (1) the Deuteronomy source, which Wise argued was not the book of Deuteronomy, but a collection of laws drawn from Deuteronomy; (2) the Temple source, which comprises instructions for the building of a huge new temple; (3) the "Midrash to Deuteronomy" source, which he identified as "a political treatise formulated by means of interpolative scriptural exegesis"[20]; (4) a Festival Calendar, which once circulated separately. Subsequent scholars have offered revisions and refinements of one or both of these theories.

In my own understanding, the Temple Scroll as found in 11QTemple[a] can be divided into four sections, plus an Introduction. The four sections are the Temple source (cols. 3-13, 30-47), the Festival Calendar (cols. 13-30), a collection of purity laws (cols. 48-51), and the Deuteronomic Paraphrase (cols. 51-66). Embedded within the Deuteronomic Paraphrase but now an integral part of it is the Law of the King (cols. 57-59).

The Temple Scroll opens with Exodus 34, which portrays Moses on Mount Sinai receiving the second covenant from God (the first having been abrogated in the golden calf incident, Exodus 32–33). This opening is appropriate for two reasons. First, in much of Exodus 34 God speaks to Moses in the first person. Thus, God's speech here sets up the entire pseudepigraphic conceit of the work: that all the laws found in the Temple Scroll were given by God directly to Moses on Mount Sinai. Since much of the legal material in the Scroll comes from the book of Deuteronomy, this setting does away with Deuteronomy's troublesome setting as a sermon of Moses on the Plains of Moab.[21] Second, since the Temple Scroll opens with the unabrogated second covenant, everything that follows (i.e., the entire scroll) is eternally legitimate,

---

18. Yadin, *Megillat ha-Miqdash,* 386, 390.
19. Wilson and Wills, "Literary Sources of the *Temple Scroll.*"
20. Wise, *A Critical Study of the Temple Scroll,* 110.
21. Weinfeld, "God versus Moses in the Temple Scroll," 178-79.

even when the author/redactor uses material from Exodus prior to ch. 34.[22] No question can be raised about the legitimacy of these regulations.

Although col. 2 uses Exodus 34 as its base text, Deut 7:25-26 also appears, interpolated between Exod 34:13 and 14. This is typical of the technique of the author/redactor, who draws in pertinent passages from outside his base text, often by the use of catchwords (in this case, "asherim" [אשרים]). As we shall see throughout the Scroll, conflation (the example here), harmonization, and supplementation are the author/redactor's main techniques for working with Scripture.

The Temple Source

As we move into the main body of the Scroll, the author/redactor betrays his priestly-levitical interests by beginning with the plan for the gargantuan temple complex he envisages in his renewed Israel.[23] The Temple source begins in col. 3; unfortunately, most of the column has not been preserved, so we do not have the introduction to the plan. Columns 3-13 contain the specifications for the temple building itself, while cols. 30-47 include the descriptions of the three courtyards surrounding the temple. The plan begins with the most sacred, the *debir* or holy of holies, where the presence of God is to dwell, and moves outward. The specifications for the temple building and its furnishings, as well as the altar and other structures around the temple, is based mainly on the tabernacle plan (Exodus 25–27). The Temple source also draws on the description of Solomon's temple (1 Kings 6) and Ezekiel's temple plan (Ezekiel 40–48), thus demonstrating the use of scriptural texts outside the Pentateuch.

The Temple source goes on to describe the various courtyards of the temple compound. A major innovation of its plan is that it calls for three square courtyards, one inside the other. No other Israelite temple in antiquity, actual or projected, had more than two courtyards. The inner court is limited to ritually pure priests and Levites, the middle court to ritually pure Israelite males over the age of 20; the outer court admitted ritually pure Israelite women, children, and proselytes. No mention is made of non-Israelites. The middle and outer courts each have 12 gates, corresponding to the 12 tribes of Israel. This aspect of the plan, in which Israel again has the full complement of 12 tribes, corresponds to the author/redactor's vision of an Israel reconstituted as a worshipping community with the temple as its focal point.

22. Brooke, "The Temple Scroll: A Law unto Itself?", 36.
23. Brooke, "The Temple Scroll: A Law unto Itself?", 41.

It is not certain whether or not the material contained in these columns ever existed independently from the Temple Scroll as a separate document or whether the author/redactor drew from existing sources to construct his unique temple plan. The existence of the fragments of 4Q365a, which include content with building specifications for a temple (frgs. 2-5), one of which (frg. 2) contains an inexact parallel to cols. 38 and 41 of the Temple Scroll, point to the latter possibility.[24]

The Festival Calendar

The Temple source is interrupted by a section that almost certainly existed independently of and prior to the redaction of the Temple Scroll: the Festival Calendar. The Calendar, which is found in cols. 13-30, was inserted by the author/redactor of the Scroll into the Temple source after the description of the temple building and its altar. Its purpose is to outline the rituals of the temple and its various festivals, including the proper sacrifices, hence its placement after the description of the altar. The Festival Calendar uses as its base text the ordinances of Numbers 28–29 and Leviticus 23, but with several striking innovations. The first is an annual festival for the ordination of priests (col. 15:3-10), in which the elders of the priests take the place of Moses, who presided over the ordination of Aaron and his sons to the priesthood in Leviticus 8. Second, rather than one First Fruits festival (Weeks, Num 28:26-31; Lev 23:15-21), the Festival Calendar calls for four: barley (col. 18:1-10), wheat (cols. 18:10–19:9), wine (cols. 19:11–21:10), and oil (cols. 21:12–23:2). The First Fruits celebrations of wine and oil also appear in 4QMMT and two other small Cave 4 manuscripts (4Q327 and 409), and the New Oil festival is mentioned, as we have seen, in 4QReworked Pentateuch. These festivals are to occur at 50-day intervals. All of these festivals occur by the principle of extension; since all of these products were to be tithed (Deut 14:22-26), it followed that there should be a First Fruits festival at the times of their harvest. The Deuteronomy text is thus harmonized, by the principle of analogy, with the festival calendar of Leviticus and Numbers.

The Festival of New Oil was followed by a Wood Festival, in which the tribes offered to the temple the wood to be used for its sacrifices (cols. 23:1–25:1). A wood offering by certain clans is mentioned in Neh 10:34; however, the only other place where a six-day Wood Festival occurs is in 4QReworked Pentateuch[c], discussed above in Chapter 3. As mentioned there, this passage

---

24. See esp. Crawford, "Three Fragments from Qumran Cave 4."

in the Temple Scroll concerning the Wood Festival is the strongest evidence that 4QReworked Pentateuch[c] was considered scriptural, at least by the composer of the Festival Calendar.

The Festival Calendar assumes the 364-day solar calendar as the calendar underlying its method of reckoning proper dates. This solar calendar, of course, is that found in the pre-Qumranic 1 Enoch and Jubilees, as well as 4QMMT and other manuscripts from the Qumran caves. This calendar, as well as the other parallels mentioned above, places the Festival Calendar and the Temple Scroll in which it is found within the Second Temple Jewish circles that produced 1 Enoch, Jubilees, and related texts.

The Purity Laws

The next section of the Temple Scroll can be isolated, although it is unlikely that it existed separately prior to the Scroll's composition/redaction. It contains purity legislation (cols. 48-51). Although Andrew Wilson and Lawrence Wills suggested that these regulations constituted a separate source,[25] the suggestion of Michael Wise concerning this section appears more plausible. Wise suggested that the author/redactor of the Temple Scroll drew on one or more existing collections of purity regulations, interlarding them into the end of the Temple source (cols. 45-47), and then continuing on to construct a separate section, the structure of which is his (cols. 48-51).[26] In this section the author/redactor reveals himself to be a "maximalist" in his approach to purity regulations, extending them to cover the widest possible sphere.[27] For example, the Temple Scroll applies the laws of Levitical purity to all the cities of Israel. In one example of this application, each city must set aside places outside the city for women who are menstruating or parturient (col. 48:16, 18; based on Lev 12:2-8; 15:19-30). In Leviticus, the regulations apply to the Levitical camp in the wilderness; the Temple Scroll extends the regulations to apply to all Israelite cities, a significant intensification.[28] The Temple City requires an even higher degree of ritual purity; for example, a man who has an ejaculation of semen during sexual intercourse with his wife is banned from entering the Temple City for three days (col. 45:11-12). The regulation is based on Moses' injunction to the Israelite men at the foot of Mount Sinai (Exod

---

25. Wilson and Wills, "Literary Sources of the *Temple Scroll*," 280.
26. Wise, *A Critical Study of the Temple Scroll*, 133-34.
27. Yadin, *Megillat ha-Miqdash*, vol. 1; Milgrom, "The Qumran Cult."
28. Japhet, "The Prohibition of the Habitation of Women," 78.

19:14-15; emphasis mine): "So Moses went down from the mountain to the people. He consecrated the people, and they washed their clothes. And he said to the people, 'Prepare for the third day; *do not go near a woman.*'" The regulation for the Sinai theophany now applies to the Temple City in perpetuity. The Damascus Document, which we have already mentioned as coming from the same priestly-levitical circles as the Temple Scroll, makes the ban on sexual intercourse explicit: "No man should sleep with his wife in the city of the temple, defiling the city of the temple with their impurity" (CD 12:1-2). It thus becomes extremely difficult, if not impossible, for a married couple to reside permanently in the Temple City. This probably accords with the wishes of the author/redactor, for whom the city in which the temple lies is not like the other cities and is to exist in a heightened state of ritual purity vis-à-vis other cities: "you shall not purify any city among your cities like my city" (col. 47:14-15[29]). Again, this approach makes the Temple Scroll compatible with such works as 4QMMT and the Damascus Document, products of a specific priestly-levitical interpretive tradition, which found a home among the Essenes, within Second Temple Judaism.

The Deuteronomic Paraphrase and the Law of the King

The final section of the Scroll is also its last, the Deuteronomic Paraphrase found in cols. 51-66. As its name suggests, the book of Deuteronomy serves as its base text, and it even follows the essential order of the core of Deuteronomy, chs. 12–26. Although Michael Wise made a complicated argument in favor of two different sources for this material, a collection of laws taken from Deuteronomy (his "D" source) and a "Midrash" to Deuteronomy,[30] the argument of Lawrence Schiffman that this section of the Scroll was composed by the author/redactor himself, using Deuteronomy as his base text, is more economical and thus more plausible.[31] While Deuteronomy serves as the base text, the author/redactor interweaves material from other parts of the Pentateuch and other books to create an interpretation of Deuteronomy that serves his theological purpose. The Deuteronomic Paraphrase, like the book of Deuteronomy itself, is concerned with life in the land, the land that surrounds the gargantuan temple that will be at the center of the nation-as-worshipping-community. By placing this section at the

---

29. See also Crawford, "The Meaning of the Phrase עיר המקדש."
30. Wise, *A Critical Study of the Temple Scroll.*
31. Schiffman, "The Deuteronomic Paraphrase of the *Temple Scroll.*"

end of the Scroll, the author/redactor has constructed a work that begins with the geographically most holy, the temple itself, to the less holy, ordinary life in the land.

The author/redactor sometimes simply quotes his base text, which appears to have been the received text of Deuteronomy. At times he harmonizes his Deuteronomy base text with another pentateuchal text or uses the base text as the trigger for a collection of laws on the same topic, drawn from other parts of the Pentateuch; at times he adds an exegetical variant for clarification or to introduce a new legal requirement; and finally he sometimes adds more extensive legal material, using his base text as a starting point.[32]

The Deuteronomic Paraphrase begins in col. 51:11-18 (after an empty space signifying an "open paragraph") with Deut 16:18 and ends, in 11QTemple[a], at Deut 23:1, although it incorporates sections of Deuteronomy 12–13 and 15 as well.[33] 4QRouleau du Temple, the oldest manuscript of the Temple Scroll, has a longer text at what is the end of 11QTemple[a], indicating that the original Deuteronomic Paraphrase may have continued past 23:1.

The Paraphrase starts, at Deut 16:18, with a discussion of just judges. This opening signals the author/redactor's concern with the moral and ritual purity of the land and the community that inhabits it, which in turn affects the purity of the temple at the center of the land. In accordance with the fiction of the Temple Scroll, God speaks in the first person. This passage gives a good illustration of the method of the author/redactor. In order to see what the author/redactor has done, I have laid out the text of 11QTemple[a] next to that of the Masoretic Text of Deut 16:18-20, with differences in the Temple Scroll in italics. I should stress that I in no way believe that the author/redactor's base text was identical to the MT of Deuteronomy. This should become clear from my remarks below. However, MT is the best default text we possess for the purposes of comparison.

11QTemple[a] 51:11-18	Deut 16:18-20 (MT)
(11) You shall appoint judges and officers in all your towns,	You shall appoint judges and officers in all your towns that the LORD your God is giving to you for your tribes,
and they shall judge the people (12) with righteous judgment. *And they* shall not	and they shall judge the people with righteous judgment. You shall not pervert justice,
show partiality *in justice, and they* shall not take a bribe, *and they*	you shall not show partiality, and you shall not take a bribe,

32. Schiffman, "The Deuteronomic Paraphrase of the *Temple Scroll*," 546-62.
33. Schiffman, "The Deuteronomic Paraphrase of the Temple Scroll," 547-48.

11QTemple^a 51:11-18	Deut 16:18-20 (MT)

shall not (13) *pervert justice,* for the bribe *perverts justice, and subverts the* the words of justice, and blinds (14) the eyes of the wise,	for the bribe
	blinds the eyes of the wise, and subverts the words of the righteous.
and causes great guilt, and defiles the House with the sin of (15) *iniquity.*	
Justice, justice you will pursue in order that you may live *and come* and inherit (16) the land that *I am* giving you *as a possession forever. And the man* (17) *who takes a bribe and perverts righteous justice shall be put to death; you shall not be afraid of him* (18) *to put him to death.*	Justice, justice you will pursue in order that you may live and inherit the land that the LORD your God is giving to you.

The author/redactor's changes to his base text begin in line 11, where he has omitted "that the LORD your God is giving to you for your tribes." This phrase is present in MT, SP, and LXX, therefore it is likely that this is a change by the redactor, perhaps to avoid the third person mention of God.

In line 12, an indication of a variant base text arises at the first occurrence of "and" in the line, where the Temple Scroll agrees with SP against MT and LXX, which do not read "and." The phrase "you shall not pervert justice," found in MT, SP, and LXX (although missing in some LXX manuscripts), has been moved two clauses down in the Temple Scroll, where it interrupts the discussion of the bribe. Further, the LXX and the Temple Scroll have the verb as a third masculine plural (יטו); the fact that this variant is present in the LXX as well as the Temple Scroll indicates that it was probably in the author/redactor's base text. The same variant occurs with the other verbs in the line, "show partiality" (יכירו) and "take" (יקחו), where the Temple Scroll agrees with LXX against MT and SP, indicating a variant base text. Finally, the phrase "in justice" is missing in MT, SP, and LXX, but is found in a parallel passage in Deut 1:17. It was probably added here by the author/redactor.

Line 13 contains the additional phrase "perverts justice" (absent in MT, SP, and LXX). This may be an allusion by the author/redactor to Prov 17:23, which reads: "A wicked man takes a concealed bribe, to pervert the ways of justice."[34]

Continuing in line 13, the author/redactor reverses the next two clauses

34. I am grateful to Mark S. Smith for bringing this allusion to my attention.

(which have the opposite order in MT, SP, and LXX) and changes the verbs from third masculine singular finite verbs (MT, SP, and LXX) to masculine singular participles. Finally, he alters "the righteous" to "justice," evidently to continue his emphasis on justice throughout the passage.

Lines 14-15 contain several new phrases that are the work of the author/redactor, punctuating the consequences of perverting justice: "and causes great guilt, and defiles the House with the sin of iniquity." The climax of this is the defilement of the temple (הבית). The temple and its purity, of course, are the chief interest of the author/redactor of the Scroll, the centerpiece of the land to which these laws apply.

Line 15 contains another illustration supporting my contention that the author/redactor was working from a base text that differed from MT. Both the Temple Scroll and the LXX contain the phrase "and you will come," which is missing from MT and SP. When a variant occurs in two ancient witnesses, it is a likely indication of an alternative received text.

Line 16 finds the author/redactor's usual change from the third masculine singular (MT, SP, LXX) to the first person, in keeping with the pseudepigraphic fiction of the Scroll.

Beginning in the middle of line 16 the author/redactor departs from his Deuteronomy base text to legislate the penalty for the unjust judge. By using the phrase "and you shall not be afraid of him" (ולוא תגורו ממנו), which occurs in Deut 1:17 concerning the importance of rendering a fair judgment even in the case of a high official and in Deut 18:22 concerning prophets, the author/redactor creates a parallel between unjust judges and false prophets. The unjust judge, like the false prophets in Deut 13:5 and 18:20, is to die, because his actions have polluted the land and thus endangered the purity of the temple.[35] This punishment is not scriptural, but for the author/redactor it follows naturally from his theological stance against impurity, both moral and ritual.[36] Thus the point of this whole introductory section is the importance of justice or righteousness, in the land that is God's gift. If Deuteronomy functions as a "second law" in the Torah, both a recap of Exodus, Leviticus, and Numbers and an enlargement of their law codes to emphasize life in the land, then the Temple Scroll is a kind of "third law," meant to recap and expand Deuteronomy by the exegetical techniques and legal interpretation of the priestly-levitical circles in which the Temple Scroll originated, for whom the temple and its purity were a primary interest. The Paraphrase, as with the rest of the Temple Scroll, is not meant to replace Deuteronomy, but to stand

---

35. Yadin, *Megillat ha-Miqdash*, 1:381; 2:227-29.
36. Regev, "Abominated Temple and a Holy Community," 261.

alongside it as an equally authoritative representation of God's revelation to Moses on Sinai. This makes the Temple Scroll an excellent legal exemplar of the category Rewritten Scripture.

A second example of the author/redactor's method, in which he uses his scriptural text as an introduction to a large block of extrascriptural text, is found in his treatment of the Deuteronomic Law of the King (Deut 17:14-20), from col. 56:12-21. Once again I will lay out the Temple Scroll text next to the MT, with differences in the Temple Scroll in italics.

11QTemple[a] 56:12-21	Deut 17:14-18 (MT)
(12) When you come to the land that *I am* giving to you, and you possess it and dwell (13) in it, and you say, "Let me set a king over me, like all the nations that are around me," (14) you shall indeed set over yourself a king whom *I* shall choose, from among your brethren you will set over yourself a king. (15) You will not *put* over yourself a foreigner who is not your brother. Only he must not (16) multiply for himself *horse,* and he must not cause the people to return (to) Egypt *for war* in order to (17) multiply *for himself* horse *or silver or gold,* since *I said* to *you* (ms), "*You* (ms) shall not (18) return in *this* (fs) way again." And he must not multiply for himself wives, lest (19) *they turn* his heart away *from me.* And silver and gold he must not multiply for himself greatly. (20) And when he sits securely on the throne of his kingdom, then *they will write* (21) for him this law in a book from before the priests . . .	When you come to the land that the LORD your God is giving to you, and you possess it and dwell in it, and you say, "Let me set a king over me, like all the nations that are around me," you shall indeed set over yourself a king whom the LORD your God shall choose, from among your brethren you will set over yourself a king. You will not be able to put over yourself a foreigner who is not your brother. Only he must not multiply for himself horses, and he must not cause the people to return to Egypt in order to multiply horse, since the LORD said to you, "You shall not return in this way again." And he must not multiply for himself wives, lest his heart turn away. And silver and gold he must not multiply for himself greatly. And when he sits securely on the throne of his kingdom, then he will write for himself a copy of this law in a book from before the levitical priests.

We immediately observe that the hand of the author/redactor is lighter here than in our first example. However, the changes that he makes (as opposed to variants in his base text) are deliberate interpretive changes that allow him to use the scriptural Deuteronomic king's law as an introduction to the longer and more polemical Law of the King that follows.

In lines 12 and 14 the author/redactor changes the third person reference to God to first person direct discourse, a change that we have come to expect.

The text of line 15 reads "you shall not put," rather than "you shall not be able to put," of MT, SP, and LXX. This may be a modernization made either by the author/redactor or his base text; it does not change the sense of the passage.

Several variants occur in line 16. The Temple Scroll reads the singular (collective) "horse" with LXX, against "horses" of MT and SP. The Temple Scroll has lost the locative or directive *he* on "to Egypt" (מצרים vs. מצרימה), a common occurrence in late biblical/Second Temple Hebrew.[37] Most importantly, the author/redactor adds "for war" to the last phrase, which changes the meaning of the prohibition against returning the people to Egypt. Trade and other peaceful activities with Egypt are evidently permissible, but war is not. It is possible that this exegetical change is the result of Judah's bad experiences with Egypt in the last years of the kingdom, especially Josiah's catastrophic defeat by Pharaoh Neco (2 Kgs 23:28-30), as well as the experiences of Judah under the Ptolemies and the Seleucids in the third and early second centuries B.C.E. The author/redactor may particularly have in mind the fact that Judaean mercenaries were serving in the armies of the Ptolemies.

The Temple Scroll agrees with LXX in having "for himself" in its base text, against MT and SP. It also adds the phrase "and silver and gold," which is an anticipation of the same phrase in line 19 (Deut 17:17). It is probable that this is a scribal error (rather than deliberate alteration) and may simply reflect the author/redactor's base text (although it does not occur in MT, SP, and LXX).[38] We find the usual change from third to first person in the reference to God. The Temple Scroll also levels through the second masculine singular referent by using "to you (masaculine singular)" (לכה) rather than "to you (masculine plural)" (לכם) of MT, SP, LXX, and 1QDeut[b]. The second masculine singular leveling continues throughout line 18. Also in line 18, both the Temple Scroll and LXX have a feminine singular demonstrative pronoun in the phrase "this way" (הזואת), rather than the masculine singular demonstrative pronoun (הזה) found in MT and SP, which indicates that the Temple Scroll or its base text took "way" (הדרך) as a feminine singular noun.[39]

In line 19 the author/redactor's hand reappears, replacing the rather vague "lest his heart turn away" (יסור) found in MT, SP, and LXX with "lest *they* turn his heart away (יסירו) *from me* (מאחרי)," thus placing the blame for

---

37. Qimron, *The Hebrew of the Dead Sea Scrolls*, 69.

38. Wise, *A Critical Study of the Temple Scroll*, 113.

39. In Biblical Hebrew, דרך can be either masculine or feminine, although it is more often construed as masculine.

the king's apostasy squarely on the wives and making the object of the apostasy clear. This is an example of clarification by the author/redactor.[40]

A most important variant occurs in line 20. The Temple Scroll contains "and they will write," rather than MT's, SP's and LXX's "and he shall write for himself" or "and it shall be written for him" (referring to the king). This variant is crucial because it removes from the king the responsibility for preserving and keeping the law and puts it in the hands of another group, presumably the priests mentioned later in the verse. The plural verb may have been in the author/redactor's base text, since it also appears in Targum Pseudo-Jonathan.[41] Nevertheless, it suits the author/redactor's exegetical purpose admirably, which is the subordination of the monarchy to the priesthood. Line 21 ends with "the priests"; it is not certain whether the text contained "the Levites," as in MT, SP, and LXX. There is space at the end of the line for the word, where we would expect it; Yigael Yadin suggests restoring it at the top of col. 57;[42] C. D. Elledge sees traces of a *waw* at the end of line 21 and thus restores "the priests *and* the Levites."[43] However, Elisha Qimron does not restore it.[44] Yadin's and Elledge's slightly different suggestions are attractive; since the Temple Scroll favors the Levites in other ways, it seems unlikely that they would be deliberately omitted here.

An exegetical crux in this passage is the meaning of "this law" which is to be written. The author/redactor of the Temple Scroll resolves that crux by a deliberate exegetical change in his base text, the deletion of "a copy" in line 21. Instead, he inserts at this point an independent document, known as the Law of the King (cols. 57-59). This Law of the King is a long continuation of the scriptural king's law. The composer of this source, which may have circulated separately prior to its inclusion in the Temple Scroll, probably had 1 Sam 10:25 in mind when he wrote, a passage in which Samuel writes down all the rights and duties of kingship. However, in the Temple Scroll it is not Samuel who is the source of these rights and duties, but God himself on Sinai. This Law of the King proceeds topically, drawing freely for its conclusions from all parts of what became the canonical scriptural text, including Kings, Chronicles, Ezra, and Psalms.[45] This extensive use of scriptural material from outside the

---

40. Although it is not unique to our author/redactor; similar understandings are found in Targum Pseudo-Jonathan and tractate *Sanhedrin;* Yadin, *Megillat ha-Miqdash*, 2:254.

41. Wise, *A Critical Study of the Temple Scroll*, 112. Some LXX witnesses have a second masculine singular verb.

42. Yadin, *Megillat ha-Miqdash*, 2:404-5.

43. Elledge, *The Statutes of the King*, 108-10.

44. Qimron, *The Temple Scroll*, 81.

45. Swanson, *The Temple Scroll and the Bible*, 117-73.

Torah is unique to the Law of the King in the Temple Scroll and bolsters the argument for its independent existence. The topics covered in the Law are:

1. The muster of the army (57:1-5)
2. The king's guard (57:5-11)
3. The royal council (57:11-15)
4. The king's marriage (57:15-19)
5. Prohibition against corruption (57:19-21)
6. Laws of war (58:3-21)
7. Curse and blessing (59:2-21)

Each subject is suggested by the Deuteronomic law of the king that introduces this section, especially as modified by the author/redactor. The overall effect of the Law of the King is to subordinate the kingship to the priesthood in all matters of governance, including the waging of war.[46] Even in marriage, the king is constrained beyond the normal Israelite male in a manner that closely resembles the marriage regulations for the high priest. The Law of the King thus fits the program of the author/redactor of the Temple Scroll by envisioning the king as a servant of the temple and priesthood in an ideal Israel.

At the end of the Law of the King the author/redactor takes up his Deuteronomic base text again by resuming Deut 17:20, "and he shall lengthen days over his kingdom, he and his descendants after him." The Deuteronomic Paraphrase then continues with Deuteronomy 18.

A third example of the author/redactor's exegetical technique, this time in the area of ritual purity, is found at the end of 11QTemple[a], col. 66:8-11, the base text of which is Deut 22:28-29. Once again, the two texts are presented in parallel columns, with the differences in the Temple Scroll in italics.

11QTemple[a] 66:8-11	Deut 22:28-29 (MT)
(8) If a man *seduces* a young woman, (9) a virgin, who is not betrothed, *and she is fit for him according to the law,* and he lies with her (10) and *it is* discovered; the man who lay with her shall give to the father of the young woman fifty silver shekels, and (11) she shall be his wife; because he has violated her, he shall not be able to divorce her all his days.	If a man *finds* a young woman, a virgin, who is not betrothed, and he seizes her and he lies with her and they are discovered; the man who lay with her shall give to the father of the young woman fifty silver shekels, and she shall be his wife; because he has violated her, he shall not be able to divorce her all his days.

46. Fraade, "The Torah of the King," 34.

Lines 8-11 contain an almost verbatim quotation of Deut 22:28-29, with some minor variants. In line 8, the Temple Scroll has "seduces" (יפתה), instead of "finds" (ימצא), of MT, SP, and LXX; the former verb is found in a parallel law in Exod 22:15, and is probably a reminiscence, possibly in the base text. The singular verb "it is discovered," in line 10 agrees with LXX against the plural of MT and SP, again a probable variant in the author/redactor's base text.

In line 9, however, the author/redactor has added a clause, "and she is fit for him according to the law," which changes the rule according to the author/redactor's concern for proper, ritually pure marriages. Even in the case of the sexual seduction of a virgin, marriage within acceptable bounds is evidently his paramount concern.[47] A similar ruling occurs in the Damascus Document (4Q270 5 16-17; 4Q271 3 9-10), which warns a father not to marry his daughter to an unfit partner: "And also he [the father] should not give her to anyone who is not fit for her, because that is 'two kinds,' an ox and an ass, and woolen and linen clothing together." The admonition in the Damascus Document is based on exegesis of Deut 22:9-11 and Lev 19:19, which contain the prohibitions against "two kinds" (כלאים). The Deuteronomy passage reads, "You shall not plant your vineyard with two kinds [of seed] lest the whole yield be forfeited, both the seed you have sown and the produce of the vineyard. You shall not plow with an ox and a donkey together. You shall not wear mixed stuff, wool and linen together." This is an example of the exegetical technique of extension; if the regulation applies to one type of thing, it applies also to another, in this case the sexual union of men and women. 4QMMT B 75-82 also likens improper marital unions between priests and laity to "mixing":

> And concerning the practice of illegal marriage that exists among the people: despite their being sons of holy seed, as it is written Israel is holy. And concerning his [Israel's] clean animal, it is written that one must not let it mate with another species; and concerning his clothes it is written that they should not be of mixed stuff; and he must not sow his field and vineyard with mixed species. Because they [Israel] are holy, and the sons of Aaron are most holy. But you know that some of the priests and the laity mingle with each other, and they unite with each other and pollute the holy seed as well as their own seed with women whom they are forbidden to marry.

Thus we have a group of texts with the same concern for "proper" marriages, all basing their ruling on exegesis of the same Deuteronomy passage. In these

---

47. The addition of this phrase has probably caused the loss (by haplography?) of "and he seizes her," found in MT, SP, and LXX, the loss of which further deemphasizes the rape.

texts we can observe the legal interests of the author/redactor and his circle through the exegetical techniques he applies in his reuse of Deuteronomy.

Conclusion

The Temple Scroll thus presents us with a legal representative of the category Rewritten Scripture, at the point along the spectrum occupied by recognizably new compositions that make the same claim to authority as the base texts they are rewriting. It has, as we have seen, a close narrative attachment to Exodus 34 through Deuteronomy 23, with special emphasis on the book of Deuteronomy. It extensively reworks that base text through various exegetical techniques, including conflation, harmonization, and clarification. It also omits blocks of material from the received text, but adds new blocks of material from other, unknown sources. The result is a new Book of the Law, meant to stand beside the received Torah as an equally authoritative representation of God's revelation to Moses on Mount Sinai. The author/redactor's claim to authority is unmistakable; however, there is no solid evidence that the Temple Scroll ever gained community acceptance by any group or at any time as a work of Scripture. Its status as Scripture remains at best uncertain.

BIBLIOGRAPHY

Bernstein, Moshe. "'Rewritten Bible': A Generic Category which has Outlived Its Usefulness?" *Textus* 22 (2005) 169-96.
Brooke, George J. "The Temple Scroll: A Law unto Itself?" In *Law and Religion: Essays on the Place of the Law in Israel and Early Christianity,* ed. Barnabas Lindars, 33-43, 164-66. Cambridge: James Clarke, 1988.
————. "The Textual Tradition of the Temple Scroll and Recently Published Manuscripts of the Pentateuch." In *The Dead Sea Scrolls: Forty Years of Research,* ed. Devorah Dimant and Uriel Rapoport, 261-82. STDJ 10. Leiden: Brill, 1992.
Crawford, Sidnie White. "The Meaning of the Phrase עיר המקדש in the Temple Scroll." *DSD* 8 (2001) 252-54.
————. *The Temple Scroll and Related Texts.* CQS2. Sheffield: Sheffield Academic, 2000.
————. "Three Fragments from Qumran Cave 4 and their Relationship to the Temple Scroll." *JQR* 85 (1994) 259-73.

Elledge, C. D. *The Statutes of the King: The Temple Scroll's Legislation on Kingship (11Q19 LVI 12–LIX 21)*. CahRB 56. Paris: Gabalda, 2004.

Fraade, Steven D. "The Torah of the King (Deut 17:14-20) in the Temple Scroll and Early Rabbinic Law." In *The Dead Sea Scrolls as Background to Postbiblical Judaism and Early Christianity*, ed. James R. Davila, 25-60. STDJ 46. Leiden: Brill, 2003.

García Martínez, Florentino, Eibert J. C. Tigchelaar, and Adam S. van der Woude. "11QTemple^b." In *Qumran Cave 11.II: 11Q2-18, 11Q20-31*, 357-409. DJD 23. Oxford: Clarendon, 1998.

————. "11QTemple^c?" In *Qumran Cave 11.II: 11Q2-18, 11Q20-31*, 411-14. DJD 23. Oxford: Clarendon, 1998.

Japhet, Sara. "The Prohibition of the Habitation of Women: The Temple Scroll's Attitude toward Sexual Impurity and Its Biblical Precedents." *JANES* 22 (1993) 69-87.

Magness, Jodi. *The Archaeology of Qumran and the Dead Sea Scrolls*. SDSSRL. Grand Rapids: Wm. B. Eerdmans, 2002.

Milgrom, Jacob. "The Qumran Cult: Its Exegetical Principles." In *Temple Scroll Studies: Papers Presented at the International Symposium on the Temple Scroll, Manchester, December, 1987*, ed. George J. Brooke, 165-80. JSPSup 7. Sheffield: JSOT, 1989.

Mink, Hans-Aage. "The Use of Scripture in the Temple Scroll and the Status of the Scroll as Law." *SJOT* 1 (1987) 20-50.

Najman, Hindy. *Seconding Sinai: The Development of Mosaic Discourse in Second Temple Judaism*. SJSJ 77. Leiden: Brill, 2003.

Puech, Émile. "4QRouleau du Temple." In *Qumrân Grotte 4.XVIII: Textes hébreux (4Q521-4Q528, 4Q576-4Q579)*, 85-114. DJD 25. Oxford: Clarendon, 1998.

Qimron, Elisha. *The Hebrew of the Dead Sea Scrolls*. HSS 29. Atlanta: Scholars, 1986.

————. *The Temple Scroll: A Critical Edition with Extensive Reconstructions*. Beer Sheva: Ben-Gurion University of the Negev Press and Jerusalem: Israel Exploration Society, 1996.

Regev, Eyal. "Abominated Temple and a Holy Community: The Formation of the Notions of Purity and Impurity in Qumran." *DSD* 10 (2003) 243-78.

Schiffman, Lawrence H. "The Deuteronomic Paraphrase of the *Temple Scroll*." *RevQ* 15 (1991-92) 543-67.

Swanson, Dwight D. *The Temple Scroll and the Bible: The Methodology of 11QT*. STDJ 14. Leiden: Brill, 1995.

VanderKam, James C., and Peter Flint. *The Meaning of the Dead Sea Scrolls*. San Francisco: HarperSanFrancisco, 2002.

Wacholder, Ben Zion. *The Dawn of Qumran: The Sectarian Torah and the Teacher of Righteousness.* HUCM 8. Cincinnati: Hebrew Union College Press, 1983.

Weinfeld, Moshe. "God versus Moses in the Temple Scroll — 'I do not speak on my own but on God's authority' (*Sifre Deut.* sec. 5; *John* 12, 48f)." *RevQ* 15 (1991-92) 175-80.

White (Crawford), Sidnie. "4QTemple?" In *Qumran Cave 4.VIII: Parabiblical Texts, Part 1,* ed. Harold Attridge, T. Elgvin, *et al.,* 319-34. DJD 13. Oxford: Clarendon, 1994.

Wilson, Andrew M., and Lawrence Wills. "Literary Sources of the *Temple Scroll.*" *HTR* 75 (1982) 275-88.

Wise, Michael O. *A Critical Study of the Temple Scroll from Qumran Cave 11.* SAOC 49. Chicago: University of Chicago Press, 1990.

Yadin, Yigael. *Megillat ha-Miqdash (The Temple Scroll).* 3 vols. Jerusalem: Israel Exploration Society, 1977; rev. Eng. ed., 1983.

CHAPTER 6

The Genesis Apocryphon

The last text I wish to discuss as an example of Rewritten Scripture is the Genesis Apocryphon. The Genesis Apocryphon lies along our spectrum at the farthest remove from the scriptural text by the simple fact that it is written in Aramaic, not in Hebrew. None of its readers could have mistaken it for the biblical book of Genesis, and it does not make the claim to authority that the composer of Jubilees or the redactor of the Temple Scroll make. As Daniel Harrington puts it, it is "an imaginative retelling of the biblical story that joins the Old Testament [sic] text and legendary material."[1]

Description of the Manuscript

The Genesis Apocryphon was discovered in Cave 1 at Qumran and exists in only one copy. It was in an advanced state of decay when it was found; when it was first examined only one large and one small fragment were peeled off from the outside of the scroll.[2] When the scroll was finally unrolled only cols. 2 and 19-22 were decipherable; these columns, along with a synopsis of the presumed contents of the other columns, were published by Naḥman Avigad and Yigael Yadin in 1956.[3] It was not until the 1990s that the remain-

1. Harrington, "Pseudo-Philo," *OTP*, 2:301, quoted in Evans, "The Genesis Apocryphon and the Rewritten Bible," 158.

2. The large fragment was eventually published by J. T. Milik as "Apocalypse de Lamech"; *Qumran Cave I*, 86-87. For a description of the various fragments and their relationship to the main scroll, see Fitzmyer, *The Genesis Apocryphon of Qumran Cave 1*, 115-17.

3. Avigad and Yadin, *A Genesis Apocryphon*. A good description of the condition of the manuscript is found on pp. 12-15.

ing columns of the scroll were deciphered with the help of advanced imaging technology.[4] With the publication of all the readable parts of the scroll, it is now possible to understand the Genesis Apocryphon as an almost complete composition (unfortunately the beginning and the end of the scroll are lost).

The paleographical date of the Scroll falls between 25 B.C.E. and 50 C.E.[5] Its language has been characterized by Joseph Fitzmyer as "Middle Aramaic," located between the Aramaic of the book of Daniel and later Western Aramaic. This places the date of the language of the Scroll from sometime in the first century B.C.E. to the first century C.E.[6] Since only one copy of this composition exists, and since the paleographical date and the date of the language of composition adhere so closely, it may be that we possess an autograph. However, it is impossible to be certain. If the Scroll is not an autograph, it is certainly close to its date of composition, which, based on its language, most likely falls in the early first century B.C.E. We find another clue to the date of composition in the sources used by the Genesis Apocryphon. As we shall see, the Genesis Apocryphon depends on sources that contained traditions also found in the books of Enoch and Jubilees. We shall argue that the Genesis Apocryphon is dependent on the actual books of Enoch and Jubilees. If we are correct, the Genesis Apocryphon's date of composition must be later than those for the earlier books of Enoch (third century B.C.E.) and Jubilees (mid-second century B.C.E.), which certainly accords with a date of composition for the Genesis Apocryphon in the early first century B.C.E. If this date of composition is accepted, then the possibility exists that the Genesis Apocryphon was composed at Qumran. However, there is nothing in its ideas or language that ties it directly to the Qumran community; as with Jubilees and the Temple Scroll, it seems to be part of a broader priestly-levitical (Essene) scribal tradition that was congenial to the Qumran community but not its product. Therefore, it may be that the Scroll was brought in from outside the community.

4. Greenfield and Qimron, "The Genesis Apocryphon col. xii"; Morgenstern, Qimron, and Sivan, "The Hitherto Unpublished Columns of the Genesis Apocryphon." See also the narration of the material in the columns by Bernstein, "From the Watchers to the Flood."

5. Fitzmyer, "Genesis Apocryphon," 302.

6. Fitzmyer, *The Genesis Apocryphon of Qumran Cave 1*, 29-37. The date Fitzmyer gives agrees with that of Kutscher, "The Language of the 'Genesis Apocryphon,'" 22. All quotations from the Genesis Apocryphon are taken from Fitzmyer, with some modifications.

Contents of the Manuscript

The Genesis Apocryphon, as its name implies, retells stories from the book of Genesis. The extant portion of the Scroll begins with narrative about the characters found in the genealogy of Genesis 5; it moves on to the story of Noah, the Flood and its aftermath (Genesis 6–10), and ends with the story of Abraham found in Genesis 12–15. Thus it follows the order of chapters in its Genesis base text. Since the final columns of the Scroll have been lost,[7] it is probable that the Scroll continued the story of Abraham. Where it ended we cannot be sure.

As James VanderKam has shown, the Genesis Apocryphon used a text of Genesis that belonged to the pre-Samaritan (which he calls the old Palestinian) text group. Further, he argues that the Genesis Apocryphon and Jubilees "presuppose virtually identical biblical *Vorlagen*."[8] Thus, three of our examples of Rewritten Scripture texts, 4QReworked Pentateuch, Jubilees, and the Genesis Apocryphon, use scriptural base texts that lean toward the harmonistic pre-Samaritan text group. This is not surprising, since the pre-Samaritan text group, as we have been arguing, is a component of the priestly-levitical line of interpretation we have been tracing throughout this book.

The composer of the Genesis Apocryphon, however, was not simply retelling (or translating) the story of Genesis. Although the book of Genesis generally serves as his base text, he uses the usual techniques of addition, omission, harmonization, re-arrangement, and anticipation to create a new, unique narrative that is unlike any other retelling of Genesis from antiquity. What is particularly striking is his use of traditions found in 1 Enoch and Jubilees; the way in which he combines traditions found in these books (and in other, more fragmentary, works from the same period) with material from Genesis (see below), particularly in the Noah cycle, indicates that he viewed these traditions as having equal authority with Genesis.

Since the Genesis Apocryphon divides itself into three separate sections, the first about the birth of Noah, the second a separate section concerning Noah with its own title, and a third about Abram, we will investigate those sections separately, paying particular attention to the composer's use of exegetical techniques. We will also give close attention to the use of the traditions found in Enoch and Jubilees throughout the text. Finally, we will discuss the Scroll as a whole and try to determine its purpose of composition and its position along the spectrum of Rewritten Scripture texts.

7. The last sheet of leather contains stitching on its right side, indicating that at least one more sheet of leather followed it.

8. VanderKam, "The Textual Affinities of the Biblical Citations in the Genesis Apocryphon," 47.

The Birth of Noah (cols. 0-5)

Columns 0-1, which are very fragmentary, contain material that seems to refer to the story of the Watchers found in 1 Enoch 1–36, based on Gen 6:1-4. The phrases "that they would not ally themselves by marriage" (col. 0, line 17) and "medicines, magicians, and sooth[sayers" (col. 1, line 11) particularly point in this direction. The columns also elaborate on the statement found in Gen 6:5: "The LORD saw that the wickedness of humankind was great in the earth, and that every inclination of the thoughts of their hearts was only evil continually." If this is the beginning of the Scroll,[9] then these columns serve as an introduction; for the author/redactor, the important events of human history begin with the descent of the Watchers. There is no room for the story of creation (Genesis 1) or the story of Adam and Eve (Genesis 2–4); the story begins with the antediluvian patriarchs, possibly Enoch himself. This is a characteristic of Second Temple Jewish literature that revolves around the figure of Enoch; the story of the Watchers signals the introduction of evil into the world, evil that is wiped out in the Flood.[10]

Columns 2-5 contain a narrative concerning the birth of Noah. The base text for this narrative is the notice of Noah's birth in Gen 5:28-29:

> When Lamech had lived one hundred eighty-two years, he became the father of a son; he named him Noah, saying, "Out of the ground that the LORD has cursed this one shall bring us relief from our work and from the toil of our hands."

However, it is immediately obvious that this short notice only supplies the occasion for the narrator to present a much longer story, which emphasizes the miraculous birth of Noah and his connections to Enoch, Methuselah, and the story of the Watchers, which is also recounted in 1 Enoch.

Column 2 opens with Noah's father, Lamech, speaking in the first person. This use of first person narrative, which occurs three more times in the manuscript in the voices of Enoch, Noah, and Abram, is an unusual feature of the Genesis Apocryphon. Lamech is somehow troubled by his newborn son, who is different in some way, and he is afraid that the child was not fathered by him, but by the Watchers or their offspring.

9. But see Morgenstern, "A New Clue to the Original Length of the Genesis Apocryphon," who suggests that the Scroll "is missing anything from 70-105 columns" from its beginning. Other than the slim evidence he cites, there is no indication that that much material was missing from the beginning of the Scroll.

10. Falk, *The Parabiblical Texts*, 43.

So then I thought to myself that the conception was from Watchers or that the seed was from the Holy Ones, or the Nephil[im]; and my mind wavered because of this child. (col. 2, lines 1-2)

This is the same scenario portrayed by 1 Enoch 106–107.[11] 1 Enoch 106 describes the miraculous appearance of the child in great detail; his hair is white like wool, his skin rose-red, and his eyes are so bright that they light up the house. This description is missing from the Genesis Apocryphon, but may appear in a small Hebrew fragment from Cave 1, 1Q19, which contains the phrases "and when Lamech saw . . . the chambers of the house like the beams of the sun . . ." (frg. 3, lines 4-5[12]). Another description of the baby Noah is evidently preserved in 4QBirth of Noah[a] ar, which mentions red hair and special moles and markings.[13] In 1 Enoch 106, Lamech goes immediately to his father Methuselah for counsel, but in the Genesis Apocryphon he first approaches his wife, Bitenosh, whose name is also given in Jub 4:28. The ensuing dialogue is one of the unique features of the Genesis Apocryphon and introduces several important themes.

In the Genesis Apocryphon Lamech's wife Bitenosh is given a voice and a character, unlike in Genesis, 1 Enoch, or Jubilees. The dialogue between husband and wife is stormy,[14] and sexual pleasure is mentioned twice (col. 2, lines 9-10, 14). Lamech, disturbed by his suspicion concerning the Watchers, is questioning his wife's sexual purity; her reassurance is not enough. The Second Temple period saw a flowering of stories in which women are major characters (Ruth, Esther, Judith, and Susannah); in all of these stories the sexual purity of the women is somehow an issue that needs to be resolved. Ruth, who seduces Boaz on the threshing floor, chooses to follow the custom of levirate marriage and thus becomes the ancestress of David; Esther in the Septuagint edition of her book declares that she loathes sharing the bed of a Gentile; Susannah is the victim of a false accusation of adultery; and Judith must reassure the elders of Bethuliah that she did not actually sleep with Holofernes before murdering him. The dialogue between Lamech and Bitenosh fits into this general Second Temple theme.[15]

11. 1 Enoch 106–107 was found at Qumran in the manuscript 4QEn[c].

12. Milik, *Qumran Cave I*, 84-86.

13. Puech, *Qumrân Cave 4.XXII*, 157-58.

14. Nickelsburg points out that the closest parallel in emotional tone is the argument between Tobit and Hannah in Tob 2:11-14; "Patriarchs Who Worry About Their Wives," 144.

15. A later example from the Enoch tradition of this general theme of the sexual purity of women is the story of the miraculous birth of Melchizedek at the end of 2 Enoch. Melchizedek, like Noah, is an unusually precocious child. The story also is related to the story of the birth of Isaac, since Melchizedek's mother and Sarah are both postmenopausal.

After the dialogue, the narrative reverts back to the same sequence as 1 Enoch 106. Lamech goes to his father Methuselah and asks him to approach his grandfather Enoch, who is the recipient of divine knowledge (col. 2, lines 20-21). The speaker changes in col. 3 to Enoch himself, who reassures Lamech about Noah's parentage and predicts the Flood. Columns 3-5 all contain Enoch's speech, which contains overlaps with the Aramaic text of 1 Enoch 106–107 as found in 4QEn^c:

ביומי ירד אבי "in the days of Jared my father" (GA, col. 3, line 3; 4QEn^c, frg. 5 ii 17; 1 En 106:13)

וכען אזל . . . הואא בקשום די לא בכדבין "and now, go . . . he is in truth and not with lies." (GA, col. 3, lines 12-13; 4QEn^c, frg. 5 ii 29-30; 1 En 107:2)

This is our strongest evidence that the Genesis Apocryphon is actually using Enoch as a source, rather than being dependent on common traditions or sources.[16] As George W. E. Nickelsburg has observed, however, Enoch's speech in the Genesis Apocryphon is much longer than that in 1 Enoch,[17] so the Genesis Apocryphon may be either using a different source or freely composing at this point. Both sections end with Methuselah returning to Lamech with the good news.

The Book of the Words of Noah (cols. 6-17)

Column 5 ends with a blank space in line 28, indicating the end of the first section. Then, in line 29, there occurs a phrase that functions as a heading for the new section: "[A Copy of] The Book of the Words of Noah." What follows features Noah speaking in the first person throughout cols. 6-15. While some of this material is loosely based on Genesis 6–9 (see below), much of it is brand new. Richard Steiner suggests that the compiler of the Genesis Apocryphon is using here an actual "Book of Noah."[18] The fact that a parallel

16. Following Fitzmyer, *The Genesis Apocryphon of Qumran Cave 1*, 139-40. Avigad and Yadin suggested that the Genesis Apocryphon was a source for 1 Enoch and Jubilees, which would mean that the date of composition for the Genesis Apocryphon would be much earlier than the date I have suggested; *A Genesis Apocryphon*, 38. García Martínez prefers the explanation of common source material; *Qumran and Apocalyptic*, 40. Falk, *The Parabiblical Texts*, is reluctant to state categorically that the Genesis Apocrypon used Enoch and Jubilees as sources, but his arguments lean in that direction; *The Parabiblical Texts*, 97-100.
17. Nickelsburg, "Patriarchs Who Worry About Their Wives," 143.
18. Steiner, "The Heading of the *Book of the Words of Noah*," 69.

phrase, "the [Book] of the Words of Enoch," occurs in col. 19, line 25, where Abram reads from it, would indicate that the compiler did have a written source in mind. Jub 21:10 mentions the "words of Enoch and . . . the words of Noah," again indicating a written source. Other fragmentary texts from Qumran, all containing traditions about Noah, also point to a widespread Noah literature at this time (1Q19; 4Q186; 4Q435-436; 4Q515; 4Q534-536; 6Q8). However, if such a source existed, it is no longer extant and its contents must remain speculative.[19] These columns also contain extensive parallels with the book of Jubilees, strengthening the argument that the author/redactor of the Genesis Apocryphon knew Jubilees and used it as a source.

Col. 6, lines 1-5 contain Noah's words of self-praise, an echo of Jub 5:19, where Noah is described as "righteous in all his ways."

> "and in the womb of her who bore me I came out for uprightness; and when I came forth from my mother's womb, I was planted for uprightness. All my days I have practiced uprightness, and I have been walking along the paths of everlasting truth; and with me the Holy One has been . . . on my tracks uprightness was settled and to warn me away from the path of deceit that leads to everlasting darkness. . . ." (lines 1-3)

The narrative continues with Noah recounting the events of his life up until the marriage of his sons (col. 6, lines 6-11). The name of Noah's wife, Emzara (col. 6, line 7), is also found in Jub 4:33; the birth of Noah's children (col. 6, lines 7-8) appears in Gen 5:32 and Jub 4:33 (where no daughters are mentioned). The mention of "jubilees" as a measure of time in col. 6, line 10 ("ten jubilees, then it came to pass for my sons to take for themselves women in marriage") also ties the Genesis Apocryphon more closely to the book of Jubilees.

Col. 6, line 11–col. 7, line 5 narrates a vision that Noah receives. This visionary capacity of Noah is not found in Genesis or Jubilees and places Noah on the same level as Enoch. It also adds an apocalyptic note to these columns.[20] Jubilees also contains apocalyptic material within its rewriting of Scripture, so its presence here in the Genesis Apocryphon should not be surprising. Noah's vision concerns the Watchers (col. 6, line 11) and the Flood, which will occur as a result of their activities (col. 6, lines 25-26). The vision is narrated by an angelic emissary (col. 6, lines 13-14):

---

19. See Werman, "Qumran and the Book of Noah," who argues against the existence of such a source.

20. Lange, "The Parabiblical Literature of the Qumran Library," 313.

"to me by the great Watcher, to me by a messenger and by an emissary of the [Great] Holy One . . . and in a vision he spoke with me; he was standing before me. . . .

Worth noting in this regard is 1 En 10:1-2, where God sends an angel to Noah to warn him of the Flood. Also, in 1 Enoch 65ff., Noah goes to his grandfather Enoch to question him concerning the wickedness of the earth. Enoch responds by showing him a vision of the Flood and its consequences, and reassuring him that he will be spared (1 En 65:12). In the Genesis Apocryphon, Noah reacts to the vision of the Flood and its consequences, including the destruction of the Watchers and his own survival, with joy, as befits a righteous man (col. 7, line 7).

Col. 7, line 19 seems to mention the building of the ark (Gen 6:14-16). Columns 8-10, which are extremely fragmentary, must have narrated the events of the Flood itself. The legible portion of col. 10 resumes with Noah and his sons praising God, presumably for bringing the Flood to an end (lines 8-10), and the ark coming to rest on Hurarat, an alternative spelling for Ararat (Gen 8:4).[21]

Lines 13-18 of col. 10 find Noah making a sacrifice, as he does in Gen 8:20-21. However, the sacrifice here is called specifically an "atoning" sacrifice (כפרת, "I atoned," line 13), as it is in Jub 6:2. Further, Noah follows the provisions for sacrifice laid out in Leviticus, first evidently (although the text is not preserved) offering a calf, then a sheep or a goat (Lev 4:27–5:26), burning the fat and sprinkling the blood (Lev 4:17, 18, 25, 30), then offering turtledoves (Lev 5:7-10). Finally, Noah offers a grain offering, as called for in Lev 6:15. All of this activity accords with Jub 6:2-3 and is meant to demonstrate that Noah, one of the righteous patriarchs, followed the prescriptions of the Torah long before Moses and Sinai. This, as we have seen, is also part of the agenda of Jubilees.[22]

Column 11 finds Noah walking the length and breadth of the land and marveling at its beauty (lines 11-12).

[Then] I, Noah, went out and walked on the land through its length and its breadth . . . upon it. There was luxuriance in their leaves and in their fruits. All the land was full of grass, herbs, and grain.

21. Falk, *The Parabiblical Texts*, 94, notes that this is the spelling preserved in SP, thus tying the Genesis Apocryphon to the pre-Samaritan tradtion. It is also the spelling found in 4QCommentary on Genesis A (chap. 7).

22. See Reeves, "What Does Noah Offer in 1QapGen X, 15?", 419, who ties this sacrifice also to the Temple Scroll.

Noah's traversal of the land is not found in Genesis or in Jubilees; however, we find the same motif in col. 21, in the Abram cycle. The purpose of the traversal seems to be to take possession symbolically of the land.

Col. 11, lines 15-19 is a paraphrase of Gen 9:1-9; God is speaking to Noah in the first person (Jub 6:4-10 follows Genesis even more closely in these lines). Column 12, line 1 mentions the rainbow (Gen 9:13; Jub 6:16). Lines 10-12 give the genealogy of Noah's sons and grandsons, which is found in Genesis 10. The Genesis Apocryphon does not follow the order of the Genesis text here; it moves the genealogies (Gen 10:1-32) in front of the incident of Noah's drunkenness in the vineyard (Gen 9:18-27). Moshe Bernstein suggests that this rearrangement is made in order to anticipate the introduction of Ham's son Canaan in Gen 9:18.[23] However, it is not clear that the Genesis Apocryphon contained these verses (the text breaks off at the bottom of col. 12), and there is some reason to suppose it did not (see below). It may simply be that the author of the Genesis Apocryphon moved the genealogies in front of the vineyard pericope so that the episode of the vineyard, in which Noah calls all his children and grandchildren together (line 16), might have a context; he wishes to make clear that there are in fact grandchildren at this point in the narrative.

The order of the sons in the Genesis Apocryphon is also different from the genealogies in Genesis. The Genesis Apocryphon gives the genealogies in the following order: Shem (line 10), Ham (line 11), and Japhet (line 12). In Genesis, the order of the sons when mentioned together is always "Shem, Ham, and Japhet" (Gen 5:32; 6:10; 7:13; 9:18; 10:1), thus implying that Shem is the firstborn. But when the genealogies are given in Gen 10:2-31, the order is reversed: Japhet is first (vv. 2-5), Ham second (vv. 6-20), and Shem last (vv. 21-31). Jubilees makes clear that Shem is Noah's firstborn (Jub 4:33) but actually gives the genealogy of Ham first, after the episode of Noah's drunkenness (7:13). Shem and Japhet's genealogies come later, in Jub 7:18-19.

The order of the genealogies of the Genesis Apocryphon may be explained by a desire to emphasize the birth order, since Shem is the ancestor of Abram, the next main character in the Genesis Apocryphon. Shem also features prominently in the vision of Noah in col. 13, where he is the first "shoot" and the source of a "righteous planting" (col. 13, lines 11-14). This may be further reason for the Genesis Apocryphon to place the genealogy of Shem first.

After the genealogies the Genesis Apocryphon moves back to Gen 9:20, where Noah plants a vineyard.

---

23. Bernstein, "Re-Arrangement, Anticipation and Harmonization," 42.

> [And] I, with all my sons, began to cultivate the earth. I planted a large
> vineyard on Mount Lubar, and in the fourth year it produced much wine
> for me. (col. 13, line 13)

The Genesis Apocryphon includes Noah's sons in this activity, and further-more locates the vineyard on Mount Lubar, which is identified in Jubilees as the mountain on which the ark rested after the Flood (Jub 5:29; 7:1).[24] Unlike the Genesis version of the story, Noah once again observes the injunctions of the Torah by observing the four-year rule and only drinks the wine in the fifth year (Lev 19:23-25; Jub 7:1-2). In Gen 9:21, Noah drinks the wine alone and gets drunk, leading to the cursing of Canaan. In the Genesis Apocryphon, Noah invites his offspring to a feast, which involves praising God (also Jub 7:3-6). It is not clear whether or not the episode of Noah's drunkenness was included in the Genesis Apocryphon. There is certainly room for it at the bottom of col. 12, and it does occur in Jubilees (Jub 7:7-13). However, one of the traits of the Genesis Apocryphon, as we shall see when we reach the Abram cycle, is to remove from the narrative all questionable elements in a patriarch's character. If the author followed this pattern in the Noah cycle, it would be unlikely that he would include the episode of Noah's drunkenness. There is no hint of it in the following columns.[25]

Columns 13-15 contain a series of visions by Noah. We have already seen that Noah is a visionary like his great-grandfather Enoch (col. 6). These visions are unique to the Genesis Apocryphon; they do not occur elsewhere in the extant literature. The vision of cols. 13-14 concerns the past and the immediate future. The rape of the earth taking place in lines 8-11 probably refers to the activity of the Watchers and their offspring.[26] An olive tree is introduced in lines 13-14:

> I turned around to look at the olive tree; for behold the olive was growing
> in height and for many hours with the glory of many leaves [and] fru[its]
> in abundance. . . .

This olive tree is probably Adam and his offspring, since it is blown down in line 17.

---

24. 1 En 10:19 mentions the planting of vineyards after the destruction of the Watchers as a sign of abundance.

25. But see Bernstein, who thinks the episode was included; "Re-Arrangement, Anticipation and Harmonization," 42. Also Falk, *The Parabiblical Texts,* 74.

26. See 1 Enoch 7, where the giants devour both wild beasts and reptiles, among other things. In ch. 8 Azaz'el teaches the use of metalwork. See also 1 En 65:6-8.

Column 14, in which an angelic interpreter is evidently speaking, introduces a cedar, identified as Noah.[27]

> [And now] lis[ten] and hear! You are the great cedar, [and] the [cedar] standing before you in a dream on the top of mountains [and h]igh grew a shoot that comes forth from it. . . . (lines 9-10)

The cedar is surrounded by three shoots that are attached to the cedar at the root (lines 11-17); these are Noah's sons. The first shoot (Shem) is praised; it will never depart from Noah (which may imply adherence to the Law), and it will bring forth a "righteous planting." The fate of the other shoots (Ham and Japhet) is not clear owing to the fragmentary nature of the lines, but there seems to be some intermarriage with Shem's offspring (lines 16-17).

Column 15's vision is apocalyptic and probably eschatological:

> And as you saw all of them; [i]f they will turn aside, the majority of them will be evil. And as you saw the man coming from the south of the land, the sickle in his hand, and the fire with him has oppressed (?) all [who serve] the [ma]jestic [Lord]. He it is who will come from the south of the land . . . and the evil. They will cast upon the fire all the reb[els . . .] and he will come between . . . (lines 9-13)

The vision features the destruction of the wicked by a divine being (the "man" in line 10; cf. Dan 7:13-14). The direction from the south is reminiscent of Judg 5:4-5, where God marches to battle from the south, or Isa 63:1, in which God comes from Edom to avenge the Israelites. Also in 1 En 1:4 God comes from Mount Sinai (the south). Without more context it is impossible to say more. The punishment by fire is found throughout apocalyptic literature; see 1 En 90:24-27; Dan 7:11; Rev 20:11-15. The four angels in line 14 may be the four archangels who are prominent in apocalyptic literature, especially 1 Enoch (see 1 En 87:2, where four angels show Enoch a vision). The vision ends when Noah awakens (line 21).

Columns 16-17 return to the Genesis narrative, with the apportionment of the land to Noah's sons and grandsons. The narrative is loosely based on Gen 10:2-32, where a few of the place names are mentioned. It is much more closely tied to Jub 8:12–9:13, which gives a detailed geographic description.[28] Some of the place names the two works have in common are the River Tina, the tongue of the sea of Egypt, the Gihon River, the Red Sea, the Euphrates,

---

27. See col. 19, where a cedar is identified as Abram.
28. Fitzmyer, *The Genesis Apocryphon of Qumran Cave 1*, 171.

and the territories of Gadir, Ashur, Aram, and Lud. The Genesis Apocryphon is probably dependent on Jubilees in these columns, although the author/redactor does not slavishly follow his source.

The Noah cycle of stories in the Genesis Apocryphon reveals a startling fact: not only is the author/redactor using Genesis as a base to create his narrative, but he is also using traditions from 1 Enoch, Jubilees, and another Noah source ("The Book of the Words of Noah"). Further, he is granting all these sources at least equal authority, and in some cases he is clearly favoring the Jubilees tradition over Genesis (see cols. 16-17 above). What was the author's purpose in creating the Noah cycle in the Genesis Apocryphon? One scenario suggests itself. If, as appears to be the case, the Qumran community held the books of Enoch and Jubilees in equal authority to what are now the canonical biblical books, including Genesis, it may be that the author wished to create a narrative that incorporated the traditions of all three (possibly four, including the hypothetical "Book of the Words of Noah") books. Since it is written in Aramaic, it was probably not meant to be taken as authoritative itself, but was meant to gather together the authoritative traditions into one continuous narrative.[29] We will see the composer/redactor's continuing use of Jubilees in the Abram cycle, but the Abram cycle demonstrates a much greater reliance on Genesis, as well as the use of other now-canonical books. For that reason we will observe a much greater use of the techniques of anticipation and harmonization than we did in the Noah cycle.

The Story of Abram (cols. 19-22)

The Abram cycle adheres more closely to its Genesis base text than the previous Noah narratives, sometimes translating the text of Genesis verbatim.[30] The influence of traditions also found in Jubilees is still strong in this section. One of the striking features of this section's style is its avoidance of the use of the Divine Name, even when it appears in the Hebrew of Genesis.

Column 18, which is now lost, must have contained the beginning of the Abram story in Genesis 11–12, since col. 19 opens with Abram already in the land of Canaan.[31] Abram is speaking in the first person, as was also the case

29. This would be like the *Diatesseron,* which combines the four canonical Gospels into one narrative.

30. This may indicate that the author/redactor is incorporating a separate source, different in style, into his composition (or that we are seeing here his own work). See also Falk, *The Parabiblical Texts,* 95-96.

31. It is unclear whether or not the Genesis Apocryphon contained the story of the tower of

for Lamech (col. 2), Enoch (cols. 3-5), and Noah (cols. 6-15). The author is deliberately paralleling the different sections, perhaps attempting to create the impression that he is excerpting a "Book of Abram" as he was quoting the "Book of the Words of Noah" in cols. 5ff.[32]

The extant portion of col. 19 opens in Bethel, where, according to Gen 12:8, Abram builds an altar and worships God. The Genesis Apocryphon puts Abram's actual words of praise in his mouth (lines 7-8), thus filling in a small gap in the scriptural narrative: "You are indeed to [me the eternal]l God." The same words of praise are found in Jub 13:8: "You are my God, the eternal God."

The Genesis Apocryphon narrative continues by giving a reason for Abram's departure from Bethel: he had not yet reached "the holy mountain." This is probably a reference to Jerusalem, which is referred to elsewhere in Scripture as God's holy mountain (Isa 11:9; 56:7; 57:13; 65:11; 66:20; Jer 31:23; Ezek 28:14; Joel 2:1; 3:17[33]). If Jerusalem is meant, this may be a subtle polemic against the old northern kingdom of Israel, which maintained a shrine at Bethel (1 Kgs 12:29-33). Or the polemic may be aimed at the Samaritans, who maintained a sanctuary on Mount Gerizim in the vicinity of Shechem. This exegetical detail is unique to the Genesis Apocryphon.

Line 9 finds Abram in Hebron, which is not mentioned in Genesis. It is, however, found in Jub 13:10, which also contains the chronological notice that Abram dwelt there two years. As we shall see below, the Genesis Apocryphon carefully follows Jubilees' chronology in the Abram cycle, which differs from the chronologies of Josephus and the rabbis.

At this point the Genesis Apocryphon greatly expands the narrative beyond what is contained in either Genesis or Jubilees.[34] Once Abram leaves for Egypt (Gen 12:10), the Genesis Apocryphon supplies some geographical detail (lines 11-13). Then, in line 14, after a blank space indicating a fresh start, Abram narrates a dream that he has.

> And I, Abram, had a dream in the night of my entering into the land of Egypt, and I saw in my dream [that there wa]s a cedar tree and a date-palm, [very beauti]ful. Some men came, seeking to cut down and uproot

---

Babel. If it did, it must have been only a short notice; see also Fröhlich, "'Narrative Exegesis' in the Dead Sea Scrolls." It is certain that the Genesis Apocryphon did not have any portion of the long narrative concerning Abram's pious youth found in Jub 11:14–12:14. Why this is so is puzzling, since the author of the Genesis Apocryphon was quite interested in Noah's miraculous childhood.

32. Nickelsburg, "Patriarchs Who Worry About Their Wives," 156.

33. Fitzmyer, *The Genesis Apocryphon of Qumran Cave 1*, 180.

34. In fact, at this point Jubilees truncates the Genesis narrative.

the cedar and leave the date-palm by itself. Now the date-palm cried out
and said, "Do not cut down the cedar, for we are both sprung from one
stock." So the cedar was spared by the protection of the date-palm, and it
was not cut [down].

This dream is unique to the Genesis Apocryphon and serves an important
function in the narrative, explaining the somewhat dubious actions of Abram
in the Genesis story. The dream also makes Abram a visionary like Noah earlier in the Genesis Apocryphon. Although Abram's dream vision is neither
apocalyptic nor eschatological like Noah's, and does not include an angelic
emissary or interpreter, there can be no doubt to the reader that it is sent by
God and foretells future events. Therefore Abram's subsequent actions are
sanctioned by God through the dream vision.

The symbolism of the dream itself seems to come from older traditions
concerning Abram and Sarai. The cedar tree is meant to be identified with the
patriarch Abram, as the earlier cedar was identified with the patriarch Noah
(col. 14, line 9). This cedar, however, is in danger. As Marianne Luijken
Gevirtz notes, "The motif of a tree being cut down occurs as a metaphor for
disaster, destruction and death in the Hebrew Bible."[35] If the cedar is Abram,
then the date palm must be Sarai. In fact, the pairing of these two trees, and
the understanding that they symbolize Abram and Sarai, seems to be an old
exegetical tradition. The pairing of the trees also occurs in Ps 92:12, "The righteous flourish like the palm tree, and grow like a cedar in Lebanon." Rabbinic
exegesis understood the pair to stand for Abram and Sarai (*M. Tanḥ. Lek
Lekha* 5; *Zohar to Genesis* 12; *Gen. Rab.* 40:1). In the case of the Zohar and *Genesis Rabbah*, the rabbis tie the psalm verse to the episode of Abram and Sarai
in Egypt (Gen 12:10-20). That is exactly the point in the Genesis narrative
where the author of the Genesis Apocryphon uses the same symbolism in the
dream vision. The Genesis Apocryphon and the rabbinic literature stem from
two different exegetical traditions; thus the fact that the same tradition appears in both corpora indicates its age.

Although Noah receives an angelic interpreter for his dream vision,
Abram interprets his own dream to Sarai. Their ensuing dialogue is like the
dialogue between Lamech and Bitenosh in that the female partner actually
speaks and has a recognizable character, the dialogue is emotionally charged,
and it has an erotic element.[36] Abram's instructions to Sarai parallel those in
Gen 12:11-13, but whereas in Genesis the subterfuge that Abram suggests may

---

35. Gevirtz, "Abram's Dream in the Genesis Apocryphon," 234.
36. Nickelsburg, "Patriarchs Who Worry About Their Wives," 152.

seem immoral, since it is simply a lie, here it is sanctioned by God. The story in Genesis also has another difficulty, which would have been troubling to Second Temple exegetes: If Sarai and Abram are in fact sister and brother, that is a violation of the laws forbidding incest between brother and sister in Lev 18:9 and 20:17. There are several different exegetical solutions to the problem: Genesis 20 (the story of Sarai and Abimelech, a doublet to the Sarai and Pharaoh story) and Jub 12:9 make Sarai Abram's half-sister. This does not solve the legal problem, since incest between half-brother and half-sister is also forbidden. According to the Targumim, Sarai is either Abram's first cousin or his niece; the latter solution would not be acceptable in the tradition of exegesis found among the Qumran Scrolls, which expressly forbids uncle-niece marriage (CD 5:7-11; 11QTemple[a] 66:15-17). None of the solutions proposed is particularly satisfactory; Jubilees chooses to pass over the whole sordid episode in silence. The Genesis Apocryphon, however, prefers to tackle it head-on. It should be noted that the Genesis Apocryphon reverses the form of Abram's request in Gen 12:13. Rather than "say you are my sister," as in Genesis, Abram instructs Sarai to say, "he is my brother," thus putting the onus for the deception on Sarai.

The identification of the pharaoh and by extension Egypt with Zoan demonstrates the author's familiarity with the Scriptures outside of Genesis. Num 13:22 identifies Zoan as a city in Egypt; in Ps 78:12, 43 Zoan is a region in Egypt ("the fields of Zoan"); and Isa 30:4 identifies Zoan as an official city in Egypt. The Genesis Apocryphon's usage is similar, although it also seems to use Zoan as a proper name for the pharaoh (lines 22, 24). Abram and Sarai stay in Egypt (evidently without her being molested) for five years; the Genesis Apocryphon is once again following the chronology of Jubilees (Jub 13:11): "And Abram went into Egypt in the third year of the week and he stayed in Egypt five years before his wife was taken from him." This chronology is at odds with Gen 12:14, which states "When Abram *entered Egypt* the Egyptians saw that the woman was very beautiful . . ." (emphasis mine).

The next lines explain how the Egyptians discovered Sarai after five years. Egyptian courtiers come to Abram seeking his wisdom (line 25). The tradition that Abram went to Egypt not merely for food but to impart his wisdom is found in various strands of Jewish tradition, including the rabbis, Josephus, and the Hellenistic writers Pseudo-Eupolemus and Artapanus.[37] The wisdom Abram imparts in the Genesis Apocryphon seems chiefly to be from "the [book] of the words of Enoch" (a title parallel to "the book of the

---

37. Feldman, "Hellenizations in Josephus' *Jewish Antiquities*," 139; Wacholder, "How Long Did Abram Stay in Egypt?", 44.

words of Noah" in col. 5, line 28). Pseudo-Eupolemus as well states that Abram's knowledge (in that case of astronomy) comes from Enoch (*Praep. Ev.* 9.17.8). In its depiction of Abram's wisdom the Genesis Apocryphon is drawing on an older tradition that filters down into several branches of interpretation in Judaism, but its particular tradition emphasizes that the wisdom comes from Enoch and that it comes in the written form of a book. These are both important elements within this priestly-levitical interpretive tradition.

The beginning of col. 20 contains the Egyptian Hyrcanus's description of Sarai's beauty.[38]

> How splendid and beautiful the form of her face, and how [plea]sant [and] soft the hair of her head; how lovely are her eyes, and how graceful is her nose; all the radiance of her face [ ]; how lovely is her breast, and how beautiful is all her whiteness! Her arms, how beautiful! And her hands, how perfect! And how attractive all the appearance of her hands! How lovely are her palms, and how long and dainty all the fingers of her hands. Her feet, how beautiful! How perfect are her thighs! There are no virgins or brides who enter a bridal chamber more beautiful than she. Indeed, she greatly surpasses in beauty all women; and in her beauty she ranks high above all of them. Yet with all this beauty there is much wisdom in her; and whatever she has is lovely.

This description is a long addition to the text of Gen 12:15, which like other scriptural passages is remarkably laconic about physical description. Moshe Goshen-Gottstein first likened this description to a form in Arabic literature known as a *wasf* ("description"), while James VanderKam demonstrated that the passage is written in poetic form.[39] The description is part of a trend toward greater interest in female beauty in Second Temple literature; many of these descriptions are remarkably prurient, given their location in religious literature. For examples, see the description of Judith's toilet in Jdt 10:3-4 and the description of Susannah in her bath and at her trial in Sus 15-18, 31-33, as well as the descriptions of the female lover in the Song of Songs. This descrip-

---

38. The use of the name חרקנוש has been taken by some commentators as an allusion to one of the Hasmonaean rulers, either John Hyrcanus or Hyrcanus II. See, e.g., Altheim and Stiehl, "Die Datierung des Genesis-Apokryphon vom Toten Meer," 214-22. However, Hyrcanus was a relatively common Greek name, and its use here is unlikely to refer to an actual historical figure. We have seen no other traces of historical allusions in the Genesis Apocryphon. The use of the name is an indication of the date of the Genesis Apocryphon in the Hellenistic period. See also Fitzmyer, *The Genesis Apocryphon of Qumran Cave 1*, 197-99.

39. Goshen-Gottstein, "Philologische Miszellen zu den Qumrantexten," 43-51; Vander-Kam, "The Poetry of *1QApGen* XX, 2-8a," 57-66.

tion of Sarai, which lingers on all the parts of her body, is part of that general trend.

Pharaoh's response confirms the divine nature of Abram's dream, for he takes Sarai (Gen 12:15) as a wife (a nonbiblical detail that gives Sarai a more honorable position) and seeks to kill Abram; this differs from Gen 12:16, where Abram is well treated. Sarai is thus justified in her falsehood, which the Genesis Apocryphon portrays her as stating directly (*contra* Gen 12:18, where Pharaoh accuses Abram after the fact of stating that Sarai is his sister).

Sarai's abduction triggers another substantial addition in the Genesis Apocryphon, which is prompted by the absence of any reaction by Abram in the Genesis text to his wife's perilous situation. It is possible to interpret the actions of Abram in Genesis as an attempt to save his own skin, with very little concern on his part for Sarai's physical or emotional well-being. The Genesis Apocryphon attempts to correct that impression, first by the addition of Abram's dream vision, which is meant to show that Abram's subsequent actions are the result of divine inspiration. Second, at the present point in the narrative, he adds several lines of material portraying Abram (and Lot) as weeping and mourning and then as praying to God for help to prevent Sarai from being defiled by illicit intercourse.

> I was not killed, but I wept bitterly — I, Abram, and Lot, my nephew, along with me — on the night when Sarai was taken from me by force. That night I prayed, I entreated, and I asked for mercy. In sorrow I said, as my tears ran down, "Blessed are you, O God most high, my Lord, for all ages. . . . Now I lodge my complaint with you, my Lord, against Pharaoh Zoan, the king of Egypt, because my wife has been taken away from me by force. Mete out justice to him for me, and show forth your great hand against him and against all his house. May he not be able to defile my wife tonight. (lines 10-15)

The afflictions God brings upon Pharaoh and his household become the result of Abram's prayer, rather than a unilateral action on God's part. Abram's praying is a detail again common to different strands of interpretation; it is found in Philo (*Abr.* 95), Josephus (*War* 5.9.380), and rabbinic Midrash.[40] The display of emotion by Abram is also typical of late Second Temple narrative literature, which, under the influence of the Hellenistic novel, places much more emphasis on the thoughts and feelings of characters than was characteristic of earlier Israelite literature. A good example is found in the Septuagint version of Esther, which takes the rather short and matter-of-fact narra-

---

40. Fitzmyer, *The Genesis Apocryphon of Qumran Cave 1*, 201.

tive of the Hebrew Esther and expands it with great emotional displays from Esther and Mordecai, which include weeping, prayers, and, in Esther's case, a dead faint. The Septuagint Esther, like the Genesis Apocryphon, was created in the first century B.C.E.[41]

God responds to Abram's prayer by afflicting Pharaoh and his household with an "evil spirit," as in Gen 12:17. The Genesis Apocryphon makes sure to state explicitly what is only assumed in Genesis; Pharaoh is not able to approach Sarai for sexual intercourse (line 17). In line 18 we find once again that the Genesis Apocryphon is following Jubilees' chronology; Sarai is in Pharaoh's palace for two years (Jub 13:11-16), whereas Josephus and the rabbis have her there for only one night.[42] Avigad and Yadin noted that the chronology of Jubilees, followed by the Genesis Apocryphon, attempts to harmonize the years of Abram's wanderings with Num 13:22: "They went up into the Negeb, and came to Hebron; and Ahiman, Sheshai, and Talmai, the Anakites, were there. *(Hebron was built seven years before Zoan in Egypt)* [emphasis mine]." According to Jubilees and the Genesis Apocryphon, Abram reaches Hebron as it is being built, and stays there for two years (col. 19, lines 9-10; Jub 13:10). He goes down to Egypt and stays there for five years, at the end of which time Zoan (i.e., Tanis) was built (col. 19, line 23; Jub 13:11-12[43]). Sarai is then in Pharaoh's house for two years, after which Abram, Sarai, and Lot leave Egypt. Both Josephus and the *Seder Olam* have completely different chronologies, although as we have noted above Pseudo-Eupolemus appears to agree with Jubilees and the Genesis Apocryphon.[44]

At the end of the two years Pharaoh seeks the aid of his wise men, magicians, and healers, who are unable to cure him. This detail, which is not part of Genesis 12, anticipates the plague and passover narrative in Exodus, in which the magicians of Egypt are unable to stop the plagues of gnats or boils (Exod 8:19; 9:11). Finally, Hyrcanus returns to Abram, seeking his aid to heal the pharaoh because he had seen Abram in a dream. These details of the dream and healing anticipate the parallel account to this Pharaoh/Sarai episode, the Abimelech/Sarah episode in Genesis 20. In that episode, God sends a dream to Abimelech in which he tells Abimelech that Sarah is Abraham's wife, not his sister. God then advises Abimelech to seek healing from Abraham. Abimelech is healed in response to Abraham's prayer. The same result is obtained here in lines 19-20. Further, once Sarai returns to Abram, Pharaoh

---

41. Crawford, "The Additions to Esther," 3:971.
42. Fitzmyer, *The Genesis Apocryphon of Qumran Cave 1*, 206.
43. Avigad and Yadin, *A Genesis Apocryphon*, 25.
44. Wacholder, "How Long Did Abram Stay in Egypt?", 48.

assures Abram that he has not touched her (line 30), as does Abimelech in Gen 20:6. These anticipations indicate that the author of the Genesis Apocryphon knew the Abimelech/Sarah episode and was attempting to harmonize the doublet. Whether or not the Genesis Apocryphon contained that Abimelech/Sarah episode is impossible to say.[45]

The role of Lot in the episode is unique to the Genesis Apocryphon. While Lot is a disreputable character in Genesis (he quarrels with Abraham, lives in sinful Sodom, and finally commits incest with his daughters), the Genesis Apocryphon seems to be attempting to rehabilitate his reputation. He weeps and prays with Abram (line 11), and now takes a leading role in freeing Sarai from Pharaoh's clutches. This rehabilitation is also at odds with Jubilees, which strongly condemns Lot (Jub 16:7-9). The reason for the rehabilitation is not apparent, except as part of a general trend in the Genesis Apocryphon to improve the character of the patriarchs.

When Pharaoh does return Sarai to Abram he also gives her gifts: "The king gave her [mu]ch [silver and go]ld, many garments of fine linen and purple, which [he laid] before her, and Hagar too" (lines 31-32). This largesse is based on Gen 12:16, but the Genesis Apocryphon has changed the sequence and the recipient: in Genesis, Abram is given gifts when Sarai is taken, whereas here Sarai is given the gifts once she is restored to her husband. Thus Abram does not benefit from Sarai's narrowly averted defilement, nor is his wealth the result of Pharaoh's generosity, since the gifts are given to Sarai. An anticipation occurs here with the mention of Hagar: in Genesis she suddenly appears in 16:1 with no explanation of how she came to be a part of Sarah's household; the author of the Genesis Apocryphon explains that by making her part of Pharaoh's gifts at this point in the narrative.[46]

After a blank space, the narrative resumes (with Abram still speaking in the first person) with the story of Genesis 13, Abram's departure from Egypt and return to Canaan. In another small anticipation, the Genesis Apocryphon notes that Lot's wife, otherwise unintroduced when she appears in Gen 19:15, also was an Egyptian (col. 20, line 34). The Genesis Apocryphon's account of Abram's sojourn in Bethel enlarges the Genesis narrative in a fashion similar to Jub 13:15-16, making it clear that Abram offered sacrifices and praise.

The separation from Lot (Gen 13:5-13) triggers the last large addition in the extant Genesis Apocryphon.

45. Bernstein, "Re-Arrangement, Anticipation and Harmonization," 49-50.

46. Bernstein, "Re-Arrangement, Anticipation and Harmonization," 44. Bernstein notes that this anticipation is evidence that the Genesis Apocryphon continued at least through the Hagar stories. The rabbis, drawing on the same tradition, claimed that Hagar was Pharaoh's daughter!

> After this day Lot parted from me because of the conduct of our shep-
> herds. He went and settled in the valley of the Jordan, and all his flocks
> with him, and I too added much to what he had. He kept pasturing his
> flocks and came to Sodom. He bought himself a house in Sodom and
> dwelt in it. I was dwelling on the mountain of Bethel, and it grieved me
> that Lot, the son of my brother, had parted from me. (col. 21, lines 5-7)

The separation itself is much shortened, with the strife between the two house-
holds summed up in the phrase "because of the conduct of our shepherds," and
Lot's choice of the Jordan valley and Sodom are narrated without comment.
What the Genesis Apocryphon does add to the narrative is Abram's generosity
towards Lot (line 6) and his grief at their parting (line 7). These narrative
choices diminish the negative aspects of Lot's character and emphasize Abram's
positive traits. In contrast, Jubilees, while also shortening this pericope, chooses
to retain the condemnation of Sodom found in Gen 13:13 and at the same time
portrays Abram as grieving over Lot's departure (Jub 13:16-18).

Gen 13:14-17 narrates God's promise of the land to Abram. The Genesis
Apocryphon takes over the pericope but introduces certain elements to present a smoother story. God commands Abram not simply to look around (Gen
13:14), but to go up to Ramath Hazor, the highest point near Bethel, and then
look around (col. 21, line 8). After this, in Gen 13:17 God commands Abram to
"Rise up, walk through the length and breadth of the land," but there is no
mention in Genesis that Abram actually fulfilled God's command. The Genesis Apocryphon remedies this deficiency by inserting several lines showing
Abram physically walking the boundaries of the land (lines 15-19). This detail
is not found in Jubilees or any other version of the Abraham story, but is parallel to the action of Noah in col. 11. The boundaries of the land are tradi-
tional, the river of Egypt (the Gihon, line 15) and the Euphrates (line 17); see,
e.g., Deut 11:24; 1 Kgs 4:21.

At this point some similarities in the Genesis Apocryphon's treatment
of the stories of Noah and Abram should be noted. Both stories have central
female characters (Bitenosh, Sarai) whose sexual purity is somehow called
into question. Both women are vindicated by the word of authority figures
(Enoch, Pharaoh), and their male relatives benefit after the vindication
(Noah, Abram). Ida Fröhlich has observed that both stories have in fact a
similar structure: (1) The sexual purity of the female character is questioned;
(2) No impurity is found; (3) The hero and his offspring receive the land.[47]
While the structures are not exactly parallel, since the author of the Genesis

---

47. Fröhlich, "'Narrative Exegesis' in the Dead Sea Scrolls," 96.

Apocryphon is more constrained in the Abram cycle by the shape of the Genesis narrative, the similarity is enough to postulate that the Genesis Apocryphon wishes to make a connection between sexual purity and the possession of the land. This connection appears in other documents which make up the Qumran library: e.g., Jubilees, as we expect, since the Genesis Apocryphon is using Jubilees itself, or the traditions found in Jubilees, as a source; the Temple Scroll, in which the laws of sexual purity are emphasized in the section of the Scroll dealing with life in the land, the Deuteronomic Paraphrase; and the Damascus Document, where fornication is one of the "three nets of Belial" (CD 4:17) and sexual impurity is one of the chief reasons for the desolation of the land (CD 5:21). As we shall see in Chapter 7, the themes of the gift of the land and the (negative) consequences of sexual impurity also surface in 4QCommentary on Genesis A. This thematic correspondence would be another reason for the appeal of the Genesis Apocryphon to the Qumran community and bolsters the case that it is a product of the wider Essene movement, with its priestly-levitical tradition of scriptural interpretation, of which the Qumran community was a part.

The Genesis Apocryphon resumes the Genesis narrative at Gen 13:18, when Abram settles at Hebron (col. 21, line 19). Again we find the Genesis Apocryphon using the device of anticipation to introduce Abram's three confederates, Mamre, Arnem, and Eshkol, who are portrayed in col. 21, lines 21-22 as sharing a feast with Abram. In Genesis, the three suddenly appear without explanation at Gen 14:13.

The Genesis Apocryphon's treatment of Genesis 14 is the closest thing we have in the manuscript to a simple translation. The narrative switches to the third person and translates Genesis 14 into Aramaic with only minor changes. The purpose of these changes is either modernization or clarification. For example, in Gen 14:1 Amraphel is identified as the king of Shinar; the Genesis Apocryphon modernizes this to Babylon (col. 21, line 23). Likewise, Ellasar in Gen 14:1 is modernized to Cappadocia (line 23). After the battle, in Gen 14:10 the kings of both Sodom and Gomorrah fall into the bitumen pits; however, in Gen 14:17 the king of Sodom, apparently hale and hearty, meets Abram in the valley of Shaveh. The Genesis Apocryphon resolves this discrepancy by having only the king of Gomorrah fall into the pits (col. 21, lines 32-33). Abram meets Melchizedek, according to Gen 14:18, in Salem; the Genesis Apocryphon glosses this with "which is Jerusalem," for clarification (line 13). In the Genesis account of Abram's encounter with Melchizedek, it is unclear who tithes to whom (Gen 14:20); the Genesis Apocryphon makes it quite clear that Abram tithes to Melchizedek (col. 22, line 17). All of these changes are minor, nothing like the substantial interventions we have noted above. What is the reason for this sudden change in character? The text of Jubilees is confused at this point: the Ethiopic version is missing the episode, but the Latin and Syriac texts preserve it. It is not substantially different from Genesis, although it is shorter. Since Jubilees does not itself alter the Genesis base text here, perhaps our author did not feel compelled to depart as far from the Genesis base text as in other parts of the narrative, since there was no need to combine his two authoritative sources. This, of course, remains speculative, but it is germane to note that when Jubilees does make an adjustment to its Genesis base text, the Genesis Apocryphon follows suit, even in small details, as in Gen 14:1, where both Jubilees and the Genesis Apocryphon change the order of the kings to put Chedorlaomer first (col. 21, line 23; Jub 13:22).

As the Genesis Apocryphon begins its treatment of Genesis 15 in col. 22, line 27, it resumes the first person narrative. It also reemphasizes the chronology it has been giving throughout the Abram cycle ("ten years have passed . . ."). This detail is not given in Jubilees, although their chronologies are the same (Jub 13:8–14:3). The Genesis Apocryphon continues with a slightly expanded account of Gen 15:1-4. The expansion (which is not in Jubilees) emphasizes Abram's wealth, evidently as proof of God's favor both in the past and continuing into the future. The Genesis Apocryphon breaks off at this point in the narrative, but as we have noted, the physical evidence of the manuscript indicates that it continued on in the Abram story. Although we cannot be certain how far into Genesis it continued, it must have continued through the birth of Isaac, since the last line of col. 22 contains the beginning of the promise of Isaac's birth.

Purpose and Authority

Our extended treatment of the Genesis Apocryphon has shown that the composer of this work used all the techniques of innerscriptural exegesis found in the category Rewritten Scripture: addition, omission, re-arrangement, anticipation, changes for clarification, and harmonization (as well as translation). The composer has relied on the now-canonical book of Genesis as one base text, but has also used Jubilees (or its traditions) as a second base text throughout his composition. In the Noah cycle he has relied heavily on the traditions of 1 Enoch as well.[48] His purpose in his composition was to com-

48. Nickelsburg has argued that even in the Abram cycle the author of the Genesis Apocryphon has used the story of the Watchers to shape the Pharaoh/Sarai episode; "Patriarchs Who Worry About Their Wives," 150.

bine the equally authoritative traditions of Genesis, Jubilees, and 1 Enoch into a whole, but he is not slavishly tied to his sources; he also feels free to use new material or older traditions not found in any of his three known sources. Although two of his base texts (and probably his other source material) were written in Hebrew, he chose to compose his work in Aramaic. Since he used Aramaic, it is unlikely that he wished to make the same kind of claim to authority for the Genesis Apocryphon as we have seen made for Jubilees or the Temple Scroll. Rather, the Genesis Apocryphon offers an example of the continuing vitality of the scribal tradition, which felt free not only to copy but to compose through rewriting. The Genesis Apocryphon also illustrates the particular biases of the priestly-levitical/Essene exegetical tradition of which the Qumran community was a part: an emphasis on the episode of the Watchers, a concern for chronology, ritual purity and impurity, especially in sexual matters, the righteousness of Israel's ancestors as evidenced by their adherence to the Law and the celebration of the cult and an emphasis on the "writtenness" of their exegetical tradition.[49] This priestly-levitical tradition binds together all the Rewritten Scripture works we have studied so far, and has its roots in the harmonistic textual tradition we have observed in the pre-Samaritan group of scriptural texts. Thus I would argue that this exegetical tradition emerges in Palestine by the third century b.c.e. or even earlier. In addition to Reworked Pentateuch, Jubilees, the Temple Scroll, and the Genesis Apocryphon, it includes 1 Enoch, Aramaic Levi, and related works and the later writings of the Qumran Essene community.

BIBLIOGRAPHY

Altheim, Franz, and Ruth Stiehl. "Die Datierung des Genesis-Apokryphon vom Toten Meer." In *Die aramäische Sprache unter den Achaimeniden,* 214-22. Frankfurt am Main: Klostermann, 1959.

Avigad, Naḥman, and Yigael Yadin. *A Genesis Apocryphon: A Scroll from the Wilderness of Judaea.* Jerusalem: Magnes, 1956.

Bernstein, Moshe J. "From the Watchers to the Flood: Story and Exegesis in the Early Columns of the Genesis Apocryphon." In *Reworking the Bible: Apocryphal and Related Texts at Qumran,* ed. Esther G. Chazon, Devorah Dimant, and Ruth A. Clements. STDJ 58. Leiden: Brill, 2005.

———. "Re-Arrangement, Anticipation and Harmonization as Exegetical Features in the Genesis Apocryphon." *DSD* 3 (1996) 37-57.

49. The word is Najman's, 62.

Crawford, Sidnie White. "The Additions to Esther: Introduction, Commentary and Reflections." In *NIB*, 3:943-72.

Evans, Craig A. "The Genesis Apocryphon and the Rewritten Bible." *RevQ* 13 (1988) 153-65.

Falk, Daniel K. *The Parabiblical Texts: Strategies for Extending the Scriptures Among the Dead Sea Scrolls.* LSTS 63. London: T. & T. Clark, 2007.

Feldman, Louis H. "Hellenizations in Josephus' *Jewish Antiquities:* The Portrait of Abraham." In *Josephus, Judaism, and Christianity,* ed. Feldman and Gōhei Hata, 133-53. Detroit: Wayne State University Press, 1987.

Fitzmyer, Joseph A. "Genesis Apocryphon." In *EDSS*, 1:302-4.

————. *The Genesis Apocryphon of Qumran Cave 1 (1Q20): A Commentary.* 3rd ed. BibOr 18B. Rome: Pontifical Biblical Institute, 2004.

Fröhlich, Ida. "'Narrative Exegesis' in the Dead Sea Scrolls." In *Biblical Perspectives,* ed. Michael E. Stone and Esther G. Chazon, 81-99. STDJ 28. Leiden: Brill, 1998.

García Martínez, Florentino. *Qumran and Apocalyptic: Studies on the Aramaic Texts from Qumran.* STDJ 9. Leiden: Brill, 1992.

Gevirtz, Marianne Luijken. "Abram's Dream in the Genesis Apocryphon: Its Motifs and Their Function." *Maarav* 8 (1992) 229-43.

Goshen-Gottstein, Moshe H. "Philologische Miszellen zu den Qumrantexten." *RevQ* 2 (1959-1960) 43-51.

Greenfield, Jonas C., and Elisha Qimron. "The Genesis Apocryphon col. xii." *AbrNSup* 3 (1992) 70-77.

Kutscher, E. Y. "The Language of the 'Genesis Apocryphon': A Preliminary Study." In *Aspects of the Dead Sea Scrolls,* ed. Chaim Rabin and Yigael Yadin, 1-35. ScrHier 4. Jerusalem: Magnes, 1958.

Lange, Armin. "The Parabiblical Literature of the Qumran Library and the Canonical History of the Hebrew Bible." In *Emanuel: Studies in Hebrew Bible, Septuagint, and Dead Sea Scrolls in Honor of Emanuel Tov,* ed. Shalom M. Paul, Robert A. Kraft, Lawrence H. Schiffman, and Weston W. Fields, 305-21. VTSup 94. Leiden: Brill, 2003.

Milik, J. T. (with Dominique Barthélemy). *Qumran Cave I.* DJD 1. Oxford: Clarendon, 1955.

Morgenstern, Matthew. "A New Clue to the Original Length of the Genesis Apocryphon." *JJS* 47 (1996) 345-47.

————, Elisha Qimron, and Daniel Sivan. "The Hitherto Unpublished Columns of the Genesis Apocryphon." *AbrN* 33 (1995) 30-54.

Najman, Hindy. *Seconding Sinai: The Development of Mosaic Discourse in Second Temple Judaism.* SJSJ 77. Leiden: Brill, 2003.

Nickelsburg, George W. E. "Patriarchs Who Worry About Their Wives: A Haggadic Tendency in the Genesis Apocryphon." In *Biblical Perspectives*, ed. Michael E. Stone and Esther G. Chazon, 137-58. STDJ 28. Leiden: Brill, 1998.

Puech, Émile. *Qumrân Cave 4.XXII: Textes araméens, premièrie parte (4Q529-549)*. DJD 31. Oxford: Clarendon, 2001.

Reeves, John C. "What Does Noah Offer in 1QapGen X, 15?" *RevQ* 12 (1986) 415-19.

Steiner, Richard C. "The Heading of the *Book of the Words of Noah* on a Fragment of the Genesis Apocryphon: New Light on a 'Lost' Work." *DSD* 2 (1995) 66-71.

VanderKam, James C. "The Poetry of *1QApGen* XX, 2-8a." *RevQ* 37 (1979) 57-66.

———. "The Textual Affinities of the Biblical Citations in the Genesis Apocryphon." *JBL* 97 (1978) 45-55.

Wacholder, Ben Zion. "How Long Did Abram Stay in Egypt?" *HUCA* 35 (1964) 43-56.

Werman, Cana. "Qumran and the Book of Noah." In *Pseudepigraphic Perspectives: The Apocrypha and Pseudepigrapha in Light of the Dead Sea Scrolls*, ed. Esther G. Chazon and Michael E. Stone, 171-182. STDJ 31. Leiden: Brill, 1999.

CHAPTER 7

4QCommentary on Genesis A

The last text we shall investigate is 4QCommentary on Genesis A (4Q252). This manuscript demonstrates within its preserved text the transition taking place in the last centuries of the Second Temple period between the implicit exegesis of Rewritten Scripture and the explicit exegesis of the "citation plus comment" form that became dominant in later Jewish and Christian commentary. Its transitional nature is demonstrated by the difficulty its editors had in arriving at a suitable title. The manuscript has appeared under the titles 4QPatriarchal Blessings and 4Qpesher Genesis A; its final editor, George Brooke, selected the title "Commentary on Genesis" as a neutral expression of its contents.[1]

Description of the Manuscript

Commentary on Genesis A consists of six fragments dating paleographically from the early Herodian period, or the last half of the first century B.C.E. According to Brooke's analysis of the physical evidence, frg. 1, col. 1 was the beginning of the text in antiquity, and the manuscript was written on a single sheet of leather, containing six columns.[2] Since the fragments preserve lines

---

1. Brooke, "252. 4QCommentary on Genesis A," 187. Three other extremely fragmentary manuscripts, 4QCommentary on Genesis B (4Q253), C (4Q254), and D (4Q254a), appear to be similar to Commentary on Genesis A since they are apparently exegetical texts concerning Genesis; see Brooke, 209-36. However, the manuscripts are so fragmentary that their contents are uncertain and no more than a minimal relationship with Commentary on Genesis A can be posited.
    2. Brooke, "The Genre of 4Q252," 162-65.

from all six columns of the manuscript, we possess the outline of the complete text, albeit with gaps and holes.

Contents

As its name suggests, the Commentary contains passages from Genesis with exegetical remarks. Like the other rewritten scriptural texts we have studied, the Commentary proceeds through Genesis in order, beginning with 6:3 and continuing (in its extant portions) with 7:10-12; 7:24; 8:3-6; 8:8-14; 8:18; 9:24-25; 9:27; 11:31; 15:9; 15:17; 18:31-32; 22:10-12; 28:3-4; 36:12; 49:3-4; 49:10; and 49:20-21. The pericopes of the Commentary assume the authority of its Genesis base text; further, the redactor/composer clearly assumed that his audience would know the text of Genesis and would recognize it as his base text.[3] However, even accounting for the fragmentary state of the manuscript, it is clear that large portions of Genesis are missing. Therefore, this is not a rewritten scriptural text like Reworked Pentateuch[b & c], which, as far as we can ascertain, do not omit much if anything from their base text. Thus, Commentary on Genesis A consists of a collection of passages from Genesis, with exegetical remarks. The question arises, can a reason(s) be discerned for the choice of these particular passages?

As the manuscript proceeds through its chosen Genesis passages, the style of commentary shifts. As we shall see below, the text begins with our by now familiar innerscriptural exegesis, in which the exegetical comments are worked into the base text to create a smooth, new text. However, in cols. 4 and 5 the style changes: the base text is quoted, and then a separate comment is given. There is no effort made to work the comment into the base text; the two are distinct. This style of commentary is known from other Qumran documents, such as the *pesharim*. We will discuss this style in more detail when we reach col. 4. For the moment, what is important is that both styles are used by the redactor/composer of Commentary on Genesis A; the work comes from a transitional period (which lasted about a century), when both styles existed and were considered valid ways of explicating the authoritative scriptural text.[4]

---

3. Brooke argues that the text-type 4Q252 uses as its base text is the text-type of the LXX; "4Q252 and the Text of Genesis," 25. Falk, however, notes that 4Q252 also preserves some readings in agreement with SP, thus making 4Q252's base text part of the Old Palestinian tradition; *The Parabiblical Texts,* 125. This would put 4Q252 into the same textual family as RP, Jubilees, and the Genesis Apocryphon.

4. Brooke, "*4Q252* as Early Jewish Commentary," 401.

The inclusion of only certain Genesis passages in the manuscript and the different styles of exegesis indicate together that the redactor/composer of Commentary on Genesis A was working from sources. Another indication that he was using sources is the title that appears before the passages from Genesis 49, "The Blessings of Jacob" (ברכות יעקוב; col. 4, line 3). Can we say anything about these sources? Do they give any clues about their origin, genre, or date? Why did the redactor/composer choose these particular sources? Were there distinct themes or questions underlying his choices? What was the purpose of the document he created from those sources?[5] As we investigate the details of Commentary on Genesis A, we will attempt to answer these questions.

The Rewritten Scripture Section (cols. 1-4, line 3)

The Commentary begins abruptly, with a rewritten version of Gen 6:3a (the scriptural base text is indicated by italics):

> "[In] the four hundred and eightieth year of Noah's life their end came for Noah *and* God *said, 'My spirit will not dwell among humanity forever,'* and their days were determined at one hundred and twenty years until the time of the waters of the flood."[6]

It is obvious from this rather abrupt beginning that the redactor/composer of Commentary on Genesis A assumes that his audience knows the story of Genesis and will recognize the name of Noah. Therefore right at its start we can state that Commentary on Genesis A is not meant as a substitute for Genesis but as a comment on it.

From its beginning, the Commentary begins to reveal certain exegetical themes, which probably guided its selection of Genesis passages. The first of these is chronology, with its subsidiary, calendar. These opening lines seek to clarify a chronological ambiguity in the received text of Genesis. Gen 6:3 reads "The LORD said, 'My spirit shall not abide[7] in humanity forever, be-

---

5. Bernstein, "4Q252: Method and Content, Genre and Sources," 76.

6. All translations of Commentary on Genesis A are taken from Brooke, "4Q252 (4QCommGen A)," with slight modifications. The scriptural text is indicated by italics.

7. ידון, a *hapax legomenon* in Hebrew (MT, SP). Commentary on Genesis A reads ידור, "dwell," which is also the reading of the LXX (καταμεινη), Targum Onkelos, Syriac, and the Vulgate. Commentary's text is part of a variant tradition attempting to make sense of the original ידון; Lim, "Biblical Quotations in the Pesharim," 72-76. For a different understanding of the variant reading, see Bernstein, "4Q252 i 2."

cause he is flesh; let his days be one hundred and twenty years." The ambiguity lies in the meaning of "one hundred and twenty years." Does it mean that God is giving humanity 120 years to repent before bringing the Flood, or is God limiting the human life span to 120 years? Opting for the latter explanation are *Gen. Rab.* 26:6, Pseudo-Philo, Josephus, and Jubilees (which, however, has "one hundred and ten" years), while the former explanation is favored by the Targums, *Gen. Rab.* 30:7, the tractate *b. Sanhedrin, Avot de Rabbi Nathan,* and the *Mekhilta de Rabbi Ishmael.*[8] Commentary on Genesis sides with these: humanity is given 120 years to live (although no mention is made of repentance) until God brings the Flood. This is demonstrated in several ways. First, the mention of the 480th year of Noah's life in line 1 indicates that this statement by God comes 120 years before the Flood, which began in the 600th year of Noah's life (line 3, Gen 7:11; see also Gen 7:6). Second, the word "their end" (קצם) appears to refer either to the offspring of the sons of God (the Watchers) and the human women (Gen 6:4) or humanity in general, both of whom would be destroyed when the Flood came. This understanding is only tentative because the pronoun does not have an antecedent in our manuscript (another indication that the redactor/composer was taking his material from another source). Finally, in lines 2-3 the text makes it clear that there is a 120-year period between God's statement and the time of the Flood. Thus the ambiguity in the Commentary's base text is clarified in several ways.

The Commentary continues through the story of the Flood in its first two columns. The focus of its exegetical interest continues to be chronology, taking the sometimes vague formulations of Genesis and making them more explicit. For example, in lines 5-10 the following chronological notations are given:

> *all the fountains of the great deep burst forth and the windows of the heavens were opened* (7:11a) *and there was rain upon the earth for forty days and forty nights* (7:12) until the twenty-sixth day in the third month, the fifth day of the week. *And the waters swelled upon the earth for one hundred and fifty days* (7:24), until the fourteenth day *in the seventh month* (8:4a) on the third day of the week. *And at the end of one hundred and fifty days the waters decreased* (8:3b) for two days, the fourth day and the fifth day, and on the sixth day *the ark came to rest on the mountains of Hurarat;*[9] *it was the seventeenth day in the seventh month* (8:4).

Note that the chronology of the Commentary is given in days and weeks, with the week being primary. Months are only mentioned in the scriptural base

---

8. Bernstein, "4Q252: From Re-Written Bible to Biblical Commentary," 6.

9. This spelling is also found in SP and the Genesis Apocryphon (see above, p. 111).

text. This indicates counting according to the solar calendar, according to which the 364-day year is divided into 52 weeks, and in which months (based on the moon, thus lunar) are secondary, if used at all. This is the same calendar used explicitly and polemically by Jubilees and is the calendar underlying the Temple Scroll and the Genesis Apocryphon. This brings Commentary on Genesis A into the circle of texts in Second Temple Judaism embracing the solar calendar. In case there was any doubt, the text makes its point specific:

> on that day *Noah went forth* (8:18a) from the ark at the end of a complete year of three hundred and sixty-four days, on the first day of the week, in the seventh . . . Noah from the ark at the appointed time, *a complete year* (emphasis mine). (col. 2, lines 2-5)

Another pericope having to do with chronology occurs in col. 2, lines 8-10, again in the style of Rewritten Scripture, which clarifies the number of years Abram stayed in Haran before departing for Canaan. So the first and most obvious theme we can isolate for the Commentary is a concern with chronology and calendar and with demonstrating that the scriptural chronological formulations can be correlated with the 364-day solar calendar.

After dealing with the chronology of the Flood story, our redactor/composer moves to an exegesis of the curse of Canaan. In Gen 9:24-25, when Noah awakes from his drunken stupor and realizes that his son Ham has humiliated him by exposing his nudity, he curses Ham's *son* (Noah's grandson), Canaan. This is an awkward moment in Genesis; why does Noah curse the presumably innocent Canaan instead of the guilty Ham? Anyone familiar with the sweep of the pentateuchal story will recognize the foreshadowing going on here: according to God's explicit, oft-repeated command throughout the Israelites' sojourn in the wilderness, the Israelites are to dispossess the Canaanites from their land and take it as their own (e.g., Deut 7:1-2). Why are the Canaanites to be so treated? Obviously, to the reader of the Torah, it is because Canaan was cursed by Noah. However, that still leaves the interpretive question of why Noah curses Canaan and not Ham in the first place unanswered. Commentary on Genesis A explains the problem by reminding the reader that prior to Noah's curse, God blessed the sons of Noah (Gen 9:1). Therefore Ham, a son of Noah already blessed by God, cannot be cursed by Noah. Thus the curse falls on Canaan:

> *And Noah awoke from his wine and knew what his youngest son had done to him. And he said, "Cursed be Canaan! A slave of slaves will he be to his brothers"* (9:24-25). But he did not curse Ham, but his son, because *God*

blessed the sons of Noah (9:1), *and in the tents of Shem may He dwell* (9:27a). (lines 5-7)

Further, the Commentary clarifies the antecedent of the "he" in 9:27a; who is to dwell in the tents of Shem? In Genesis, the antecedent could be God, or it could be Japhet. In the Commentary, *God* is the clear antecedent; it is God who dwells in the tents of Shem, that is, with Shem's descendants, the Israelites (also Jub 7:12).

That this rewritten scriptural passage is followed immediately by a passage referring to God's promise to Abraham (lines 8-13; Gen 15:7-21) is not accidental, for the land God promises to Abraham is the land occupied by the accursed Canaan. Thus the land and its rightful possession appears to be another topic of concern to the redactor/composer.[10]

The remainder of Commentary on Genesis A concerns those who are dispossessed in one way or another by bad behavior and, conversely, the good behavior of the righteous, which results in various rewards. The unrighteous include the cities of Sodom and Gomorrah (col. 3, lines 1-6; Genesis 18–19; the specific verses quoted are Gen 18:31-32). The commentary written into the scriptural text uses a by now familiar technique; the commentator uses verses from Deuteronomy to explain why Sodom and Gomorrah were completely wiped out. Deut 13:13-17 contains the law concerning the city condemned for apostasy, which falls under the ban (חרם) and must be destroyed as an offering to God. Deut 20:10-14 concerns enemy towns that refuse to make peace; the males are to be killed, but the women and children may become booty. The commentator understands that these Deuteronomic laws apply retroactively to Sodom and Gomorrah; God thus follows his own laws of war. The consistency of the Pentateuch (and God) is assumed, and the Law is in effect during the patriarchal period.[11]

Another unrighteous example is Amalek, found in col. 4, lines 1-3. The governing Genesis verse is 36:12, which contains a genealogical notice of Amalek's birth: "*Timna was the concubine of Eliphaz, the son of Esau. And she bore* him *Amalek.*" There is no hint in this Genesis verse that Amalek will become the great enemy of Israel, whom God commands Israel to destroy utterly (Exod 17:8-16; Deut 25:17-19). The antagonism between Amalek and Israel continues in the reign of Saul (1 Sam 14:48; 15:2-35) and even resurfaces in

---

10. Brooke, "The Thematic Content of 4Q252," 45.

11. Brooke, "The Deuteronomic Character of 4Q252," 122-24, 135. Recall Chapter 4 on Jubilees, where a similar (and systematic) retrojection of the Law into the antediluvian and patriarchal periods occurs, and Chapter 6 on the Genesis Apocryphon, where the patriarchs are likewise portrayed (although much less systematically) as observing the Law.

the book of Esther, in which Haman, the enemy of the Jews, is a descendant of Agag, the king of the Amalekites.[12]

The Genesis commentator wishes to remind his audience of God's implacable opposition to the unrighteous Amalekites, and their final destruction. The commentary follows the brief Genesis notice with a mention of Saul's war with the Amalekites: "he whom Saul destroyed." The statement about Saul is surprisingly neutral, even positive, considering that Saul is roundly condemned in 1 Samuel for failing to destroy the Amalekites.[13] Next, the commentator attaches the command from Deut 25:19, with the intriguing addition of "in the latter days" (באחרית הימים): "as he spoke to Moses, 'In the latter days *you will wipe out the memory of Amalek from under the heavens*.'" This phrase refers to the eschatological age and frequently occurs in texts from Qumran, especially those identified as sectarian.[14] Its appearance here in Commentary on Genesis A is the first hint of anything that ties this text more closely to the Qumran community than to the general priestly-levitical circles we have seen at work in the other Rewritten Scripture works we have discussed. It also indicates an eschatological interest on the part of the redactor/composer of the Commentary, who chose this passage for inclusion in his document.[15] As part of the unrighteous, the Amalekites will be dispossessed of their very lives, according to our Commentary; this may not have yet happened, but it will, since the contemporary time is "the latter days," the eschatological age. Not only does the reach of God's law stretch back into the patriarchal period (Sodom and Gomorrah), it stretches forward into the eschatological age.

The righteous are not neglected in the Rewritten Scripture portion of Commentary on Genesis A. Besides Abram's sojourn in Haran and God's promise of the land found in col. 2, lines 8-14, the binding of Isaac, or the Aqedah (Genesis 22), is mentioned in a very fragmentary context in col. 3, lines 6-9. This is, of course, the ultimate righteous act on Abraham's part. Isaac's blessing of Jacob is referred to in col. 3, lines 12-15, so that all three righteous ancestors of Israel, the recipients of the promise of the land, appear in the Commentary. It would seem that these righteous ancestors are to be contrasted with the unrighteous Ham/Canaan, Sodom and Gomorrah, and

---

12. The book of Esther was not found at Qumran, and it is likely that the community living there rejected it. The curse of Amalek, of course, was known throughout Judaism in the postexilic communities.

13. Falk notes that 4Q252's use of scriptural passages from outside the Pentateuch indicates a developing sense of the "unity and sufficiency" of Scripture; *The Parabiblical Texts,* 138.

14. Steudel, "אחרית הימים in the Texts from Qumran," 227.

15. Brooke, "The Deuteronomic Character of 4Q252," 128.

Amalek, thus cementing Israel's claim to the land and its status as righteous. In the next section of the Commentary the real identity of the righteous and their role in the eschatological age will be revealed.

The "Citation Plus Comment" Section

Col. 4, line 3 introduces a new section of the Commentary with the title "The Blessings of Jacob." This title refers to the poem in Gen 49:2-27, which Jacob recites to his children on his deathbed. In Genesis, Jacob prefaces the poem with the comment, "Come together that I may tell you what is to befall you *in the latter days*" (באחרית הימים; Gen 49:1), the same phrase found in the Commentary in the passage concerning Amalek. While Jacob's statement is omitted from our Commentary, where the poem begins with the Blessing of Reuben (Gen 49:3), its presence in line 2 above ties the two sections together and indicates that, like the curse on Amalek, the blessings of Jacob are to be fulfilled "in the latter days," the eschatological age, the time of the redactor/composer and his audience. The exegesis that follows not only anticipates events of the eschatological age, but also interprets those events in ways typical of works peculiar to the Qumran community.

An important characteristic of this section that ties it most closely to other Qumran community documents is the use of the phrase *pishro* (פשרו), "its interpretation is," found in col. 4, line 5. This phrase signals a particular exegetical form found uniquely in Qumran scrolls, and called "pesher-type" exegesis. It is a type of "citation plus comment" exegesis, in which a line (verse, phrase, lemma) of scriptural text is quoted, followed by a separate exegetical comment that includes interpretation and explanation. The comment is often atomized; that is, the individual words of the scriptural citation are commented on separately. Although a form of the word "pesher" often occurs, it is not necessary; the personal or demonstrative pronoun (הוא or היא, המה or הנה) works as well.[16] The exegesis often, but not always, concerns contemporary events or persons familiar to the Qumran community (but not to us!) and is set in the eschatological age, construed as the present time of the interpreter. Because of this eschatological theme, "pesher-type" exegesis is usually applied to prophetic texts or texts understood as prophetic, such as the Psalms or other ancient songs.[17]

Pesher-type exegesis occurs in several different types of compositions.

16. Lim, *Pesharim*, 50.
17. Dimant, "Pesharim, Qumran," 248.

"Continuous *pesharim*" are commentaries on entire (or large portions of) scriptural books (scrolls), proceeding verse-by-verse through the authoritative text and interpreting it. Fifteen continuous *pesharim* have been discovered at Qumran.[18] "Thematic *pesharim*" gather scriptural citations concerning a particular theme from a variety of texts and interpret them to illuminate the chosen theme. For example, 11QMelchizedek concerns the redemptive activity of the mysterious figure Melchizedek; it gathers quotations from Leviticus, Deuteronomy, Isaiah, Psalms, and Daniel and relates them all to Melchizedek.[19] Finally, a pesher-type comment may appear in another genre, interpreting a specific scriptural verse for the purpose of the larger work. In the Damascus Document, one of the major rulebooks found at Qumran, cols. 3:20–4:5 contain a pesher-type exegesis of Ezek 44:15:

> As God ordained for them by the hand of the prophet Ezekiel, saying, *The Priests, the Levites, and the sons of Zadok who kept the charge of my sanctuary when the children of Israel strayed from me, they shall offer me fat and blood.* The *Priests* are the converts of Israel who departed from the land of Judah, and (the *Levites* are) those who joined them. The *sons of Zadok* are the elect of Israel, the men called by name who shall stand at the end of days.

Commentary on Genesis A uses pesher-type exegesis in its last three columns, once using the term *pishro* and after that the demonstrative pronoun (היא, col. 5, line 2; המה, col. 5, line 3; היא, col. 5, line 6). The first pesher-type comment occurs in the Blessing of Reuben (Gen 49:3-4). The citation plus comment reads,

> "*Reuben, you are my firstborn and the first fruits of my strength, excelling in dignity and excelling in power. Unstable as water, you shall no longer excel. You went up onto your father's bed. Then you defiled it.*" "*On his bed he went up!*" Its interpretation is that he reproved him for when he slept with Bilhah his concubine.

The interpretation clarifies the incident alluded to in the quotation, referring to Reuben's violation of Bilhah narrated in Gen 35:22. In the Genesis narrative Jacob "finds out" that Reuben has violated Bilhah, but appears to do nothing about it. However, Reuben's punishment is revealed in the later (non)blessing, where Jacob takes away Reuben's status as firstborn. The *pesher* is meant to make the connection between the earlier narrative and the blessing clear.

---

18. Lim, *Pesharim*, 15.
19. Lim, *Pesharim*, 14.

The next blessing extant is the Blessing of Judah, in col. 5. The lemma from Gen 49:10a is given, *"the scepter shall not depart from the tribe of Judah."* This is only a partial quotation of the verse; since the second half of the verse, "nor the ruler's staff (מחקק) from between his standards/feet," is featured in the interpretation, the opening quotation may serve as a reminder or a memory jog for the entire verse. First, however, the interpretation begins with the citation of another scriptural text, "When Israel rules *there will not be cut off one who occupies the throne for David"* (Jer 33:17). This second scriptural text illuminates the first, making it plain that the scepter belonging to Judah resides in the Davidic house, and that situation obtains as long as Israel rules (an enigmatic phrase interpreted below).

The Commentary then goes on to a pesher-type exegesis of both scriptural citations.

> For *"the staff"* is the covenant of the kingship; the thousands of Israel are "the *standards"* until the coming of the messiah of righteousness, the shoot of David. For to him and his seed has been given the covenant of the kingship of his people for everlasting generations, which he kept[. . .] the Law with the men of the community, for [. . .] it is the congregation of the men of [. . .] he gave/Nathan. . . .

Interestingly enough, the first word it interprets, "staff" (מחקק), does not occur in the half-verse of Gen 49:10 that is written out but in the second half of the verse, which is omitted. "Staff" is interpreted as the "covenant of kingship," bringing to mind the whole history of the Davidic house. The second word that is interpreted, "standards" (הדגלים), involves an interesting textual variant. Again, the word "standards" does not appear in the half-verse which is quoted, but in the second half, that is, "and the ruler's staff from between his standards/feet." The SP text of Gen 49:10b reads "his standards" (דגליו), but in the MT/LXX versions we find the staff between Judah's *feet* (רגליו). The difference between דגל, "standard," and רגל, "foot," is in the initial consonants, which are paleographically very close and in some hands almost identical. Sometime in the transmission history of Genesis, a *dalet/resh* (ד/ר) or *resh/dalet* (ר/ד) exchange took place, resulting in the variant readings.[20] Did the commentator (whether the redactor/composer of Commentary on Genesis A or his source) use a pre-Samaritan text of Genesis? Was he aware of both variants and deliberately chose the one that best suited his interpretation? None of the Qumran Genesis manuscripts preserve this verse, so we

---

20. Brooke, "Some Remarks on 4Q252 and the Text of Genesis," 7-8.

cannot be certain if both readings were extant at Qumran at all. If the commentator did use a pre-Samaritan reading, that choice would be further evidence that 4QCommentary on Genesis A belonged within the priestly-levitical/Essene line of interpretation we have been tracing throughout this book. In any case, the use of "standards" enables the commentator to pursue a particular eschatological line of interpretation.

The word "standards" occurs frequently in the War Scroll, the eschatological text *par excellence* of the Qumran community, in which each division of the congregation gathered for battle has its own standard, e.g.,

> On the standard of the Thousand they shall write, "The Wrath of God is Kindled against Belial and against the Men of his Company, Leaving no Remnant," together with the name of the chief of the Thousand and the names of the leaders of its Hundreds. (1QM, col. 4)

Here in the Commentary the standards are identified with the "thousands of Israel," thus in a military context, and are also associated with the eschatological, messianic age. This brings Commentary on Genesis A further into the orbit of specifically Qumran concerns and motifs, as did the use of the phrase "in the latter days."

There is yet another phrase in this section of the Commentary that points to its belonging to the Qumran community, and that is the phrase "men of the Community" (אנשי היחד). The word "Community," or *yaḥad,* is one of the self-designations in Qumran texts for their own group. The word appears often in the Community Rule (1QS), from which it takes its name (for examples of the entire phrase, see 1QS 5:1; 6:21; 7:20; 8:11; 9:7, 10). The Community Rule is one of the central sectarian texts in the Qumran collection, and its phraseology can be labeled specifically Qumranian. The phrase's appearance here in Commentary on Genesis A marks this section as a product of the group at Qumran. This does not mean that both sections of the document are or began as sectarian, but in its final form, the product of the redactor/composer, the work becomes sectarian. This leads to the conclusion that the redactor/composer did not see any inherent contradiction among his sources, although only one of them, the "citation plus commentary" section, was a product of his own subgroup, the Qumran Essenes, within Judaism.

Even though this final section can be labeled sectarian, it fits in with the themes we have discerned in the earlier section of the document. The theme of the righteous and the unrighteous, and the dispossession of the unrighteous, continues. Reuben is, of course, unrighteous, and he is dispossessed of his status as firstborn. It is possible that the redactor/composer selected Reuben as his example of unrighteousness in this section because his situation is similar to that of Esau, mentioned in passing in col. 4, line 1 (*"Timna was the concubine of Eliphaz, the son of Esau"*). Esau also lost his status as firstborn to Jacob (Gen 25:27-34), the very Jacob who is blessed by Isaac at the end of col. 3, lines 12-14, and who is speaking the blessings in cols. 5 and 6. If this understanding is correct, the redactor/composer neatly connects the sections of his document by these multiple allusions to the underlying Genesis narrative.

Judah is the righteous example, who receives and retains the covenant of kingship. The understanding of the identification of Judah is gradually revealed in the *pesher* exegesis. The focus narrows throughout the column from the tribe of Judah, to David, to the "branch of David" (the messiah), who is somehow connected to the men of the Community. The men of the Community are associated with the Law, which we may assume they keep/study/observe.[21] The Community is thus the true heir of Judah, the heirs of the covenant of kingship, and, even more, the heirs of the promise made to the righteous Abraham, Isaac, and Jacob. If we are correct that the main focus of the promise in this document is the gift of the land, then the Community is the rightful inhabitant of the land, the true Israel, from whom "the scepter shall not depart."[22] Thus the theme of the righteous and the unrighteous, which begins with the righteous Noah, whose righteousness is underlined by the fact that the events of the Flood can be correlated to the (proper and correct) solar calendar, culminates in the men of the Community, the heirs of the promise, the true Israel.

Conclusion

Commentary on Genesis A offers us a glimpse into the world of scriptural interpretation in the Qumran community in the last century of the Second Temple period. It is the work of a redactor/composer, who combined different sources to create a document concerned with the interpretation of Genesis from a sectarian point of view. In the creation of his document, however,

---

21. Schwartz, "The Messianic Departure from Judah," 259-65. Notice the passage in the Community Rule concerning the command of constant Torah study: "And where the ten are, there shall never lack a man among them who shall study the Law continually, day and night, concerning the right conduct of a man with his companion. And the Congregation shall watch in community for a third of every night of the year, to read the Book and to study the Law and to bless together" (1QS, col. 6).

22. Also Brooke, "The Thematic Content of 4Q252," 56-57, and Falk, *The Parabiblical Texts*, 137.

he did not hesitate to use earlier, nonsectarian sources, i.e., the Rewritten Scripture section of the work. He just put those sources to work in the service of his interpretive goal. He also did not hesitate to use sources that used different exegetical techniques. We can thus say that it is the interpretation, rather than the technique, which was uppermost in the mind of our redactor/composer. Both techniques of interpretation were valid in this time period, and both could be pressed into service of his ultimate goal, the right interpretation of Scripture. The mixing of the two styles signals a transition period; the exegetical technique of rewriting Scripture is fading as the notion of a scriptural text fixed in all its details gains ascendancy. The latest example of a Rewritten Scripture text is the *Liber Antiquitatum Biblicarum* of Pseudo-Philo, written in the late first century C.E. In the same period, the proto-rabbinic text becomes the accepted scriptural text in Judaism, and all other text forms disappear from the Jewish community.[23] At that point the "citation plus commentary" form of exegesis that we see here in 4QCommentary on Genesis A, as well as other manuscripts from the Qumran collection, takes over completely.

BIBLIOGRAPHY

Bernstein, Moshe J. "4Q252: From Re-Written Bible to Biblical Commentary." *JJS* 45 (1994) 1-27.

―――. "4Q252: Method and Content, Genre and Sources." *JQR* 85 (1994-95) 61-79.

―――. "4Q252 i 2: לא ידור רוחי באדם לעולם: Biblical Text or Biblical Interpretation?" *RevQ* 16 (1993-95) 421-27.

Brooke, George J. "252. 4QCommentary on Genesis A." In *Qumran Cave 4.XVII, Parabiblical Texts, Part 3*, ed. Brooke, James C. VanderKam, John J. Collins, et al., 185-207. DJD 22. Oxford: Clarendon, 1996.

―――. "4Q252 (4QCommGen A)." In *Exegetical Texts*, ed. Donald W. Parry and Emanuel Tov, 106-11. The Dead Sea Scrolls Reader, Pt. 2. Leiden: Brill, 2004.

―――. "4Q252 as Early Jewish Commentary." *RevQ* 17 (1996) 385-401.

―――. "The Deuteronomic Character of 4Q252." In *Pursuing the Text: Studies in Honor of Ben Zion Wacholder*, ed. John C. Reeves and John Kampen, 121-35. Sheffield: Sheffield Academic, 1994.

―――. "The Genre of 4Q252: From Poetry to Pesher." *DSD* 1 (1994) 160-79.

―――. "Some Remarks on 4Q252 and the Text of Genesis." *Textus* 19 (1998) 1-25.

23. Tov, "Scriptures: Texts," 836.

————. "The Thematic Content of 4Q252." *JQR* 85 (1994) 33-59.

Dimant, Devorah. "Pesharim, Qumran." In *ABD*, 5:244-51.

Falk, Daniel K. *The Parabiblical Texts: Strategies for Extending the Scriptures Among the Dead Sea Scrolls.* LSTS 63. London: T. & T. Clark, 2007.

Lim, Timothy H. "Biblical Quotations in the Pesharim and the Text of the Bible — Methodological Considerations." In *The Bible as Book: The Hebrew Bible and the Judaean Desert Discoveries,* ed. Edward D. Herbert and Emanuel Tov, 71-79. London: British Library and New Castle, DE: Oak Knoll, 2002.

————. "The Chronology of the Flood Story in a Qumran Text (4Q252)." *JJS* 43 (1992) 288-98.

————. *Pesharim.* Companion to the Qumran Scrolls 3. London: Sheffield Academic, 2002.

Schwartz, Daniel R. "The Messianic Departure from Judah (4QPatriarchal Blessings)." *TZ* 37 (1981) 256-66.

Steudel, Annette. "אחרית הימים in the Texts from Qumran." *RevQ* 16 (1993-95) 225-46.

Tov, Emanuel. "Scriptures: Texts." In *EDSS*, 2:832-36.

CHAPTER 8

Conclusion

As we have moved through the chapters of this book, and the compositions located at various points on our spectrum of Rewritten Scripture texts, a pattern of interpretation has emerged, one characterized by the technique of innerscriptural exegesis. A specific exegetical tradition has also emerged, which we have labeled the priestly-levitical/Essene line of interpretation. These two phenomena are related to one another. After discussing the two in order, we will collect the evidence we have presented throughout this book that demonstrates their relationship.

Innerscriptural Exegesis

The goal of innerscriptural exegesis is to clarify and interpret the scriptural text from within. As we have seen, the scribes who embraced the task of innerscriptural exegesis (as opposed to those scribes who elected to copy the manuscript in front of them word-for-word) began with the technique of harmonization.

Harmonization was an accepted technique of interpretation in Second Temple Judaism, and has produced what we have called the pre-Samaritan group of pentateuchal manuscripts. Harmonization smoothes out perceived differences between two parallel texts by importing details from one text into another or by changing one text to avoid any apparent differences with the other. All changes are made only by reference of one scriptural text to another; no "outside" texts are used. The technique of harmonization assumes the existence of a known, authoritative work, fixed in its general form, which comes from an earlier, "classical" period in ancient Israel. The details of the text, as we have seen, however, are not yet fixed in the Second Temple period, and can be altered to produce a "better" text. The motivation to harmonize stems from the notion that the text of Scripture is perfect, and perfectly harmonious. Thus, the act of harmonization produces a text of Scripture that achieves the goal of what it is already thought to possess, perfection. A well-harmonized text should have no gaps or holes, nothing that could create questions or doubts in the mind of the reader.

Chapter 2 discussed in detail the pre-Samaritan group of texts. The members of this group are not exact copies of one another, but they utilize the same techniques of harmonization and content-editing. This group of pentateuchal manuscripts generated at least one canonical text, the Samaritan Pentateuch. In addition, the group of Jews living at Qumran, a subset of the wider Essene movement, accepted these harmonized pentateuchal manuscripts as having the same authority as their shorter, proto-rabbinic counterparts.

At the next location on the spectrum we encountered the Reworked Pentateuch group of texts (Chapter 3). This group of texts used the techniques of harmonization and content-editing familiar from the pre-Samaritan group, but they went a step further by adding material into the scriptural text from "outside." The Reworked Pentateuch group is not, as far as we can determine, creating a "new" text of the Pentateuch, but simply carrying the techniques of harmonization and content-editing found in the pre-Samaritan group to their logical extreme, in the process producing what we have called a "hyper-expansive" text. Although it is practically assured that certain exemplars of this group (4Q364, 4Q365) claimed the same level of scriptural authority as other pentateuchal manuscripts (whether pre-Samaritan, proto-rabbinic, or nonaligned), what remains uncertain is whether this claim to authority ever gained community acceptance. This question continues to constitute a gray area in the study of Rewritten Scripture.

The next three examples we studied, Jubilees (Chapter 4), the Temple Scroll (Chapter 5), and the Genesis Apocryphon (Chapter 6), are located farther along the spectrum of Rewritten Scripture, at the point where new works are created. These three compositions are separate and distinct from the books of the Pentateuch on which they are based, but not so far removed that we cannot still recognize a clear connection to their base text(s). All three compositions use various exegetical techniques to achieve their goals: harmonization, content-editing, conflation, modifications and additions for clarification, and addition through exegesis. What results is a new composition, separate from the base text(s), with a distinct theological agenda, which can be expressed through narrative (Jubilees, the Genesis Apocryphon) or legal rulings (the Temple Scroll).

Although none of these works are meant to replace their authoritative base texts as Scripture, Jubilees and the Temple Scroll make a claim to equal authority with the Torah (the Genesis Apocryphon does not make such a claim). Both works make this claim via their narrative settings: both are set on Sinai at the time Moses is given the Law. Jubilees claims to be dictated to Moses by an angel of the presence, while God himself gives the Temple Scroll to Moses. In the case of Jubilees, we offered compelling evidence that the community of Jews living at Qumran, and by extension the entire Essene movement, accepted and validated this claim. In the case of the Temple Scroll, however, our evidence for community acceptance is ambivalent, and we must be content for the Temple Scroll's scriptural status to remain uncertain.

Finally, we investigated a work that combines the technique of innerscriptural exegesis with the "citation plus commentary" style of inter-pretation, 4QCommentary on Genesis A. We noted that the author/redactor used at least one source, an otherwise unknown Rewritten Scripture text, when composing his brief commentary. The evidence of this text implies that the practice of rewriting Scripture for the purpose of exegesis was even more common than our direct evidence suggests. 4QCommentary on Genesis A also demonstrates that in the first century B.C.E. interpreters had no difficulty combining both forms of commentary to achieve their exegetical goals. We also noted, however, that after the first century B.C.E. the technique of innerscriptural exegesis began to die out. We explained this development as owing to the widespread acceptance of a fixed, unchangeable textual tradition and the ascendancy of the shorter, proto-Rabbinic textual tradition. Exegesis through manipulation of the text itself became unacceptable. Exegesis from the late first century C.E. on became separate from the text of Scripture.

The Priestly-Levitical/Essene Exegetical Tradition

As we have traced the phenomenon of rewriting Scripture through these vari-ous compositions, we have discovered a distinct line of interpretation that we have called priestly-levitical, and that we identified with the Essene movement in Second Temple Judaism. This line of interpretation is most easily recog-nized in Jubilees, the Temple Scroll, and the Genesis Apocryphon, the three Rewritten Scripture texts that are separate compositions, distinct from their base texts. Certain emphases are noticeable in these works: the use of, or po-lemic in favor of, the solar calendar, an emphasis on the Levites and the choice of Levi as priest, the idea that the Law was observed by the righteous ancestors before Moses, and that the priestly office was exercised by at least some of the righteous ancestors (Enoch, Noah, Abraham, Isaac) before Levi. We also noticed the prominence of the Watcher myth, the extension of temple purity to everyday life, and the notion of a written tradition of revelation from God, beginning with Enoch and stretching down through the generations.

As we have observed, these themes do not only appear in Jubilees, the Temple Scroll, and the Genesis Apocryphon, but they also occur in a large group of texts, all of which are found at Qumran: the Enoch literature, Aramaic Levi and its related texts, the Noah literature, the Damascus Document, and 11QMelchizedek, as well as others. Many of these works, including Jubilees, the Temple Scroll, the Enoch literature, and Aramaic Levi, were composed before the settlement at Qumran was founded and are evidence of a wider, pre-Qumran existence for this line of interpretation. Some of these texts, such as the Enoch literature and Jubilees, continued to flourish after the Qumran community disappeared, again testifying to a wider circulation in antiquity. Thus we can say that this priestly-levitical line of interpretation appeared sometime in the early Second Temple period, flourished in the third and second centuries B.C.E., and found a congenial home in the Essene movement, a subset of which settled at Qumran. This priestly-levitical/Essene line of interpretation developed at least partly in opposition to themes characteristic of another group of texts, often labeled proto-Pharisaic, which include an emphasis on Moses *and* Aaron, the Zadokite priesthood alone, the notion that temple purity was separate from the purity requirements for ordinary life, and the use of a lunar calendar. Works in this group include Tobit, the Wisdom of Jesus ben Sira, and Judith. The two groups are not exclusive, as attested by the presence of Tobit and ben Sira among the manuscripts found at Qumran, as well as common traditions between the Qumran texts and later rabbinic works, but they do contain clear and sometimes polemical differences.[1]

The group at Qumran developed from this priestly-levitical/Essene interpretive line a more stringent set of theological emphases, including a more pronounced dualism, end-time eschatology, and a distinct set of sectarian terms.[2] We have seen this sectarian emphasis surfacing in the last composition we studied, 4QCommentary on Genesis A.

I would like to argue for a broadening of the priestly-levitical/Essene constellation of texts to include those texts at the beginning of our spectrum,

---

1. See also Nickelsburg, "The Books of Enoch at Qumran"; Stone, "Enoch, Aramaic Levi and Sectarian Origins"; Jackson, *Enochic Judaism*; and Boccaccini, *Beyond the Essene Hypothesis.*
2. Newsom, "'Sectually Explicit' Literature from Qumran."

the pre-Samaritan and the Reworked Pentateuch groups of texts. Both of these groups are free from any specific polemical emphasis and do not share the main interpretive concerns of the priestly-levitical/Essene works, such as the solar calendar or the prominence of the Watcher myth. As such, any group in the Second Temple period could have adopted them as their scriptural text.[3] However, these particular Rewritten Scripture groups seem to have found a home in the Essene movement, as shown by their distribution in the caves at Qumran and the use of texts from the group as the base texts for Jubilees and the Genesis Apocryphon. At the same time, these Rewritten Scripture groups were rejected by the group of Jews (probably centered in the Jerusalem temple) that eventually chose the proto-rabbinic texts as the scriptural text of the Jewish community after the fall of the Second Temple.

The reason that the pre-Samaritan and Reworked Pentateuch groups of texts are found among the priestly-levitical/Essene circles is because of their emphasis on written, innerscriptural exegesis. For the Jews who produced these texts, Scripture is written and as such contains everything necessary to understand the will of God. It does not need a separate, oral tradition of interpretation. Now, this may mean that when gaps or problems are discovered in the text they are corrected, so that Scripture is made the perfect and harmonious whole it is meant to be, and in the end actually is. That is legitimate exegetical work, performed by learned scribes. These harmonized texts then become the basis for the next step in exegetical activity, taking the scriptural text and working with it to create new, written documents that present in a more obvious way the particular concerns of the priestly-levitical/Essene movement. This too is considered legitimate exegetical work, because it grows out of a written text and results in a written text. These written texts claim to contain a scribal tradition extending back through Moses all the way to Enoch. By placing the pre-Samaritan and Reworked Pentateuch groups at the beginning of the spectrum, the spectrum that culminates in the Rewritten Scripture works that belong to the priestly-levitical/Essene movement in Second Temple Judaism, we can discern a basis for their approach to Scripture and its interpretation: Scripture is written, harmonious, and perfect, and its exegesis begins with a written text and ends with a written text. A clear line can be traced backward from one written text to another, all the way back (as it is claimed) to the antediluvian period. Thus, all of these texts along our spectrum, from the pre-Samaritan group through the Temple Scroll, are able to make the same claim of divine authorization.

---

3. One exemplar of the pre-Samaritan group was in fact selected by the Samaritans as their scriptural text and became the Samaritan Pentateuch.

We have noted, however, that as these Rewritten Scripture works became further and further removed from their base texts, their claim to divine authority was accepted only by a narrower and narrower segment of the Jewish community. The pre-Samaritan group, at one end of the spectrum, was most widely accepted as authoritative; the Temple Scroll, at the other end of the spectrum, presents only very slight evidence that it was ever accepted by any Jewish group at any time as divinely authorized. The Genesis Apocryphon makes no claim to divine authority at all. The effect is like a stream traveling through a channel that constantly narrows; this stream of inner-scriptural interpretation finally comes to an end in the final decades of the Second Temple period.

This stream began with the work of anonymous scribes, laboring in the early centuries of the Second Temple period, who produced the texts we now label the pre-Samaritan and the Reworked Pentateuch groups. It continued with the learned scribal exegetes or author/redactors who produced Jubilees, the Temple Scroll, and the Genesis Apocryphon. We can now trace the exegetical tradition within which these anonymous scribes and author/redactors worked, beginning with the harmonized texts of Scripture and culminating in the works they themselves produced in the late Second Temple period. Their erudition and scribal skills live on in these texts, which we are now able to locate within one stream of tradition among the many that make up Second Temple Judaism.

BIBLIOGRAPHY

Boccaccini, Gabriele. *Beyond the Essene Hypothesis.* Grand Rapids: Wm. B. Eerdmans, 1998.

Jackson, David R. *Enochic Judaism: Three Defining Paradigm Exemplars.* London: T. & T. Clark, 2004.

Newsom, Carol A. "'Sectually Explicit' Literature from Qumran." In *The Hebrew Bible and Its Interpreters,* ed. William H. Propp, Baruch Halpern, and David Noel Freedman, 167-87. Winona Lake: Eisenbrauns, 1990.

Nickelsburg, George W. E. "The Books of Enoch at Qumran: What We Know and What We Need to Think about." In *Antikes Judentum and Frühes Christentum,* ed. Bernd Kollmann, Wolfgang Reinbold, and Annette Steudel, 99-113. BZNW 97. Berlin: de Gruyter, 1999.

Stone, Michael E. "Enoch, Aramaic Levi and Sectarian Origins." *JSJ* 19 (1988) 159-70.

Index of Modern Authors

Index of Scripture and Other Ancient Literature